CCCC Studies in Writing & Rhetoric

REMIXING COMPOSITION

REMIXING COMPOSITION

A HISTORY OF MULTIMODAL WRITING PEDAGOGY

Jason Palmeri

Southern Illinois University Press
Carbondale and Edwardsville

Publication partially funded by a subvention grant from the Conference on College Composition and Communication of the National Council of Teachers of English.

Library of Congress Cataloging-in-Publication Data
    Palmeri, Jason, 1977–
    Remixing composition : a history of multimodal writing pedagogy / Jason Palmeri.
      p. cm. — (Studies in writing & rhetoric)
    Includes bibliographical references and index.
      ISBN-13: 978-0-8093-3089-8 (pbk. : alk. paper)
      ISBN-10: 0-8093-3089-X (pbk. : alk. paper)
    1. English language—Rhetoric—Study and teaching. 2. Report writing—Study and teaching (Higher) 3. Multimedia systems. I. Title.
    PE1404.P354 2012
    808'.0420711—dc23   2011027518

CONTENTS

ACKNOWLEDGMENTS

I AM A WRITER who first and foremost invents through spoken conversation. While I alone am listed as the author on the title page, this book might better be seen as a kind of remixed collage of the voices of the many colleagues, mentors, friends, and students who helped me *talk out* my ideas.

Within the past few years, numerous colleagues have generously read and offered invaluable feedback about portions of this manuscript. I am especially grateful for the powerful, inventive conversations I have shared with Sara Webb-Sunderhaus, Catherine Braun, Kate Ronald, Cynthia Lewiecki-Wilson, Rebecca Dingo, Cheryl Ball, Abby Dubisar, Ben McCorkle, and Donna Strickland.

I also would like to express my appreciation to Miami University for providing me with an Assigned Research Appointment in fall 2009, which enabled me to complete substantial portions of this manuscript. While at Miami, my thinking about multimodal writing pedagogy has been deeply influenced by my ongoing reflective dialogue and inventive collaboration with our wonderful community of teachers. Although there are too many people to name, I want to offer special thanks to Heidi McKee (who has been instrumental in founding and sustaining the Digital Writing Collaborative, which enables my work) as well as to Bre Garrett, Denise Landrum, James Porter, John Tassoni, Wioleta Fedeczko, Kerrie Carsey, Karryn Lintelman, Lisa Blankenship, Brent Simoneaux, Caroline Dadas, Aurora Matzke, Kevin Rutherford, Stephanie Weaver, Abby Dubisar, Amir Hassan, Jeremy Withers, Mandy Watts, Dom Ashby, Joe Burzynski, Gina Patterson, Chanon Adsantham, Scott Wagar, Lance Cummings, Alison Welch, Leigh Gruwell, Kelly Quinn,

Anita Mannur, Julie Minich, Melissa Kerwood, Ben Wetherbee, and Ann Updike. I also would like to offer a shout-out to Stephen Kostyo, Elizabeth Garrett, Bizzy Young, and the many other exceptional undergraduate students at Miami whose creativity, passion, and critical engagement continue to inspire me. And, finally, a special thanks to my colleague, Kate Ronald, for her invaluable mentoring, friendship, and good humor.

I first began my work recovering composition's multimodal heritage while teaching and completing a dissertation at Ohio State University—though my thinking and writing have evolved substantially since then. First and foremost, I would like express my deep gratitude to my dissertation advisor, Cynthia Selfe, for her enthusiastic encouragement, her insightful questioning, her invaluable feedback, and her generous willingness to welcome me into her office whenever I needed, once again, to talk out my ideas. I also would like to acknowledge Scott DeWitt for first convincing me to make a multimodal turn in my teaching and for providing me with an inspirational model of reflective, process-based, multimodal pedagogy. I also would like to thank Brenda Brueggemann and Beverly Moss for their invaluable support and advice as well as for their strong encouragement of my attempts to begin thinking beyond the binaries and "master narratives" of our field. Thanks too to Richard Selfe for teaching me much about sustaining multimodal writing programs.

Looking even farther back, I also would like to acknowledge Miriam Wallace (my undergraduate thesis advisor at New College of Florida) for her generous support of my earliest attempts to theorize a pluralist model of English studies pedagogy. As a busy tenure-track faculty member, Miriam took the time to meet with me individually nearly every week over multiple years to quite literally help me *talk* my way into the academy. And, for that, I am eternally grateful.

I also would like to express my great appreciation to Studies in Writing & Rhetoric series editor Joe Harris, as well as to reviewers Janet Carey Eldred and Adam Banks, for their enthusiastic encouragement, helpful advice, and insightful revision suggestions. Many thanks as well to Kathleen Kageff, Kristine Priddy, and Wayne

Larsen of Southern Illinois University Press for their keen editorial acumen and speedy work shepherding this manuscript into print. Finally, I would like to thank my family—my parents, Marcia and Rick, and my sister, Laura—for their love, compassion, support, practical wisdom, and good humor. I dedicate this book to them.

REMIXING COMPOSITION

Prologue

THERE ONCE WAS A TIME *when I knew what it meant to be a compositionist.* In calling myself a compositionist, I was identifying as a person who possessed specialized disciplinary knowledge about the teaching of writing—specialized disciplinary knowledge of strategies for teaching students to engage reflectively and critically in the complex, multifaceted process of composing *words.* Although I tried to design unique assignments and activities for my writing classes, I was also always conscious that my pedagogical practices had been strongly informed by the tradition of composition scholarship. When I emphasized revision and peer response in my writing classes, I knew that I was drawing on the foundational insights of composing process research from the 1960s, 1970s, and 1980s. When I asked students to experiment with freewriting as an invention technique, I recognized that I was following in the footsteps of Peter Elbow (among others). When I taught students to consider how they were using appeals to ethos, pathos, and logos in their writing, I realized that I was indebted not only to Aristotle's *Rhetoric* but also to Corbett's *Classical Rhetoric for the Modern Student.* When I engaged students in writing critically about social hierarchies of race, class, and gender, I felt confident that I was continuing in the tradition of other compositionists—critical, feminist, and cultural studies pedagogues—who had long been arguing that the teaching of writing is a political act.

There once was a time when I knew what it meant to be a compositionist... and then everything changed. Influenced by talking with colleagues as well as by reading scholarly literature, I began to pay attention to the ways that proliferating digital technologies were transforming what it meant to compose (Ball; DeVoss, Cushman, and Grabill; Ellertson; Kress; New London Group; Sorapure; Wysocki). I began to realize that it was not enough to teach students to compose alphabetic texts alone—that students needed to be able to compose with images, sounds, and words in order to communicate persuasively and effectively in the twenty-first century (D. Anderson; Ball and Hawk; Diogenes and Lunsford; Hocks; Journet; C. Selfe, "The Movement"; Shipka, "Multimodal"; WIDE). I began to recognize that many students were already composing multimodal texts outside of school, and that my composition courses might lose relevancy if I didn't make a space for composing beyond the printed word (George; C. Selfe and Hawisher; Vie; Yancey). I also began experimenting with multimodal composing myself, crafting Flash animations, videos, and websites for both activist and academic purposes.

Drawing on this experience, I started teaching composition students to produce a wide range of multimodal texts, including digital videos, audio essays, collages, animations, and websites. For the most part, I found that students really enjoyed and appreciated the opportunity to move beyond the alphabetic. I was often quite impressed with the multimodal texts that students produced, and I found that we often had great class discussions about the rhetorical choices that students made in their digital composing. I began singing the praises of multimodality to anyone who would listen.

Except there was one problem . . . *I no longer knew what it meant to be a compositionist.*[1]

Back when I was just teaching students to compose words, I had the confidence that I was drawing my pedagogy from a substantial tradition of composition scholarship—that all of my pedagogical practices were grounded in my specialized disciplinary knowledge about the teaching of alphabetic writing. But when I started teaching students to compose multimodal texts, I felt like I was leaving the composition tradition behind—venturing into uncharted pedagogical waters. What kind of specialized disciplinary knowledge could I *as a compositionist* possibly claim about composing with images and sounds? When colleagues (both in English and outside it) asked what qualified me to teach multimodal composing, how could I respond?

And, furthermore, how could I responsibly integrate multimodal composing into a first-year composition course that was still institutionally mandated to focus on teaching alphabetic literacy? Was it really possible to incorporate multimodal composing in a way that actually enhanced rather than detracted from the teaching of alphabetic writing?[2]

As I wrestled with these questions, I found myself revisiting many of the classic texts of composition theory from the 1960s, 1970s, and 1980s, looking for moments where past compositionists had attempted to draw connections between alphabetic, auditory, and visual modalities of composing. As I did this rereading, I came to understand that multimodality was not a new fad in composition studies—that compositionists have attempted, at least since the 1960s, to articulate alphabetic writing as a multimodal process that shares affinities with other artistic forms of composing (Berthoff; Corbett; Costanzo; Elbow; Emig; Flower and Hayes; Kytle; Murray; Shor; Smitherman; Williamson). I started to believe that embracing multimodal composing did not necessarily mean turning away from the composition tradition—that in fact the composition tradition had many insights to offer contemporary digital multimodal teachers. In other words, I began to realize that it was time for me (and indeed for the field) to develop a new narrative of *what it means to be a compositionist*—a narrative that would include the many ways that past writing teachers engaged multimodality. It is this new narrative that I begin telling here.

Introduction: Reseeing Composition History

I've always been fascinated by the deleted scenes that are often included as an extra on DVDs. When I click through the deleted scenes, I usually try to figure out why the director (or editor) ultimately decided not to include them. In many cases, I end up surmising that the scenes were cut because they didn't seem to fit the main narrative of the film—because they got in the way of the primary story the director wanted to tell. As a teacher of writing and as a historian of composition, the deleted scenes remind me that the stories we tell are always partial and incomplete. Composing is not just a process of creation; it's a process of deletion too. Whenever we attempt to craft a coherent, focused argument, we invariably end up leaving a great deal of interesting material on the cutting-room floor. Whenever we attempt to remember a particular aspect of our past, we always end up forgetting another.

In the past few years, advocates of the "multimodal turn" in composition have been telling a very persuasive and influential narrative about the past, present, and future of composition studies—a narrative about how and why we must move beyond our historic focus on alphabetic literacy. We can hear this story in the words of Cynthia Selfe, who asserts that "if our profession continues to focus solely on the teaching of alphabetic composition—either online or in print—we run the risk of making composition studies increasingly irrelevant to students engaging in contemporary practices of communicating" ("Toward" 72). We can hear this story in the words of Andrea Lunsford, who argues that "where writing once meant *print* text—black marks on white paper, left to right and top to bottom—today 'writing' is in full Technicolor; it is nonlinear and alive with

4

sounds, voices, and images of all kinds" (xiii). We can hear this story in the words of Kathleen Yancey, who proclaims that "literacy today is in the midst of tectonic change"—that writing teachers must move beyond the printed word to meet the needs of a digital generation of students who "compose words and images and create audio files on web logs (blogs), in word processors, with video editors and Web editors" (298). Over and over again, we encounter the same refrain: alphabetic literacy is our past; multimodal composing is our future.

In many ways, this multimodal progress narrative has been productive and useful. Indeed, I must note that it was this story of progress—of change—that first motivated me to experiment with teaching audio and video composing in my writing classes. Yet, as much as I find this progress tale to be compelling, I have also come to recognize that it—like all stories—necessarily conceals as much as it reveals. In emphasizing the importance of responding to "new" audio and video technologies, scholars have inadvertently deleted from view many of the vivid multimodal scenes that flourished in our field's past. In our headlong rush to embrace multimodality as a radically "new" phenomenon, we've forgotten for example about the many multimedia textbooks of the early 1970s that were designed to appeal to the multimodal interests of students who had grown up watching television; we've forgotten about Ann Berthoff's exploration of the similarities between alphabetic and visual composing; we've forgotten about Geneva Smitherman's powerful critique of the conventional privileging of print forms of knowledge in the academy; we've forgotten about Donald Murray's fascination with the intersections between photography and writing. These scenes, and many more, have all ended up on the cutting-room floor as scholars have focused on telling stories about how our contemporary digital "moment . . . is like none other" (Yancey 297).

Challenging the persistent notion that composition has historically been focused on words alone, I seek in this book to recover how past compositionists in the 1960s, 1970s, and 1980s studied and taught alphabetic writing as an embodied multimodal process that shares affinities with other forms of composing (visual, aural, spatial, gestural). Looking closely at the ways that past compositionists responded to the "new media" of their day, I demonstrate that writing teachers have a substantial history of engaging analog technologies for composing moving images and sounds—a history that predates the rise of the personal computer or the development of the graphical web. In recovering composition's multimodal heritage, I ultimately aim to: 1) demonstrate the unique disciplinary expertise that compositionists bring to multimodality; 2) elucidate how multimodal composing can enhance students' invention and revision of alphabetic texts; 3) offer a critical perspective about both the overexuberance and the fear that often accompany the introduction of new technologies in our field.

Although many scholars have written histories of the development of composition studies since the 1960s (Berlin, *Rhetoric and Reality*; Crowley; Ede; Foster; Harris, *A Teaching*; Henze, Selzer, and Sharer; Hawk; Miller), most of this important scholarship has not addressed the crucial role of multimodality and new media within the development of composition as a field. Recently, however, a few scholars have begun the work of uncovering composition's multimodal heritage. In *Talking, Sketching, Moving,* Patricia Dunn seeks to excavate the "lost threads in composition theory" (30) that privileged multimodal ways of knowing the world. In particular, Dunn briefly articulates ways that such foundational theorists as Emig, Britton, and Elbow explored multimodal strategies for teaching alphabetic writing (30–32), and she also suggests that compositionists pay attention to the multimodal teaching strategies embedded in Paulo Freire's critical pedagogy (37–57). While Dunn's work offers a useful starting place for recovering our field's multimodal heritage, she still tends to place most of her emphasis on critiquing the field of composition for having historically privileged alphabetic literacy over other forms of knowing. Similarly, in *Composition as a Happening,* Geoffrey Sirc analyzes the ways that a few 1960s and 1970s compositionists (Deemer; Lutz) developed multimodal composing pedagogies inspired by avant-garde art traditions, but he focuses most of his attention on critiquing the field's broader failure to engage the visual arts. Similarly, in his recent *Rhetoric of Cool,* Jeff Rice offers a useful critique of how compositionists failed to attend to "new media" in 1963, but he ignores the ways that writing teachers began to engage new media in the latter part of the decade.

In a 2002 *CCC* article, Diana George provides a fascinating history of the contested role of visual production in composition pedagogy over the past forty years. Although George focuses mostly on articulating how compositionists have marginalized visual production, she also briefly points to a few interesting moments in composition history when visual production played a more central role. Similarly, in a recent article in *CCC*, Cynthia Selfe offers a powerful history of the interrelation of aurality and writing instruction. Although Selfe usefully discusses a few ways that compositionists experimented with audio composing in the 1970s and 1980s, she ultimately argues that "the history of writing in U.S. composition instruction, as well as its contemporary legacy, functions to limit our professional understanding of composing as a multimodal rhetorical activity" ("Movement" 617). In other words, Selfe (following Dunn, Rice, George, and Sirc) primarily focuses on how the multimodal turn requires us to *move beyond* our past. In contrast to these previous histories, this book seeks to demonstrate the unique disciplinary heritage that compositionists bring to the study and teaching of multimodal composing, highlighting ways that contemporary writing teachers can productively build on our field's past.

The recovery of our multimodal disciplinary heritage is particularly pressing because we are not the only scholars in the university who have a stake in multimodality. As Pamela Takayoshi and Cynthia Selfe have noted, writing teachers often question whether or not multimodal composing should fall under their purview: "Why should English composition faculty teach multimodal composing? Shouldn't we stick to teaching writing and let video production faculty teach video? Art and design faculty teach about visual images? Audio production faculty teach about sound?" (8). Similarly, Patricia Dunn has related that many composition teachers have resisted her efforts to argue for the value of multimodal ways of learning because they feel that it seems "absurd to question an overemphasis on words in a discipline whose raison d'être is, like no other discipline, for and about writing" (15). In order to contest the notion that the study of alphabetic text is the sole raison d'être of composition studies, it's necessary that we recover the oft-forgotten ways that multimodal theories of process figured prominently in the disciplinary formation of our field.

Although I am focusing much of this book on articulating compositionists' disciplinary expertise in multimodal composing, I should note that I also believe that we have a great deal to learn from other allied arts fields. My goal in recovering compositionists' multimodal heritage is most pointedly *not* to protect our "turf" or "claim" on multimodality, but rather to articulate what specifically we have to bring to wider interdisciplinary collaborations. Furthermore, I recognize that numerous scholars have questioned whether or not composition can be or should be termed a "discipline" at all (Harris, "Undisciplined"; Smit), especially since the teaching of writing is a concern that transcends all disciplines in the university. Nevertheless, I would note that even when scholars call for interdisciplinary writing programs, they still tend to perceive a role for an administrator or mentor with special expertise in composition studies who can offer guidance and support to other writing teachers. In other words, even if we resist conceptualizing composition as a traditional discipline, we still retain a need to articulate what particular expertise composition specialists bring to the table in interdisciplinary environments.

In addition to making an argument about disciplinary expertise, I also seek in this book to demonstrate ways that multimodal composing can enhance the teaching of alphabetic writing. After all, even if we grant that it is important to teach students to craft multimodal texts, we must recognize that alphabetic writing remains a valued form of composing that we are institutionally and professionally mandated to teach. As a result, it makes sense to highlight ways that multimodal composing activities can contribute to students' invention and revision of alphabetic texts. In making this claim, I am building on the recent work of scholars who have articulated the crucial role that multisensory, mental imagery plays in alphabetic writing, helping us recognize that the composing of alphabetic text is a profoundly multimodal process (Childers, Hobson, and

Mullin; Dunn; Fleckenstein; J. Murray; Smagorinsky). For example, Kristie Fleckenstein has argued for a pedagogy of "imageword," which recognizes that imagery and alphabetic literacy are deeply intertwined—that "imagery, the incarnation of meaning in various modes and modalities, is inextricable from the linguistic manifestation of meaning and thus inextricable from the ways in which linguistic meaning is taught" (2). Seeking to help students draw connections between visual production and alphabetic reading and writing, Fleckenstein outlines various ways that visual composing activities can help students respond to reading and invent ideas for writing. Ultimately, Fleckenstein argues that alphabetic writing and reading are deeply embodied, multisensory processes; in this sense, alphabetic writing is always already multimodal.

Further demonstrating ways multimodal pedagogy can enhance the teaching of alphabetic writing, Patricia Dunn's *Talking, Sketching, Moving* outlines numerous "aural, visual, kinesthetic, and spatial" activities that teachers can employ to help students gain "metacognitive distance" on their written work (11). Recognizing that people all have diverse strengths and limitations in their ability to learn through alphabetic, auditory, visual, and kinesthetic means (Gardner, *Frames*), Dunn argues that it is important to provide students with multiple sensory pathways—sketching, audio journals, walking a draft—for inventing and revising alphabetic texts. Challenging the notion that multimodal composing necessarily detracts from students' learning of alphabetic writing, Dunn suggests instead that multimodal activities can in fact help many students come to write stronger alphabetic products.

In making these powerful and important arguments for multisensory approaches for teaching writing, Fleckenstein, Dunn, and other multimodal advocates tend to suggest that composition as a field has (with a few exceptions) been focused largely on words alone—that we have historically studied and taught the process of alphabetic writing as an almost wholly monomodal affair. In contrast, this book seeks to demonstrate that compositionists have a substantial history of developing and enacting multisensory approaches for enhancing students' development of alphabetic writing skills. Long before the contemporary multimodal turn, compositionists have been articulating the deep interconnections between seeing and writing—experimenting with ways that visual composing can help students both generate ideas for and consider revisions of alphabetic texts (Berthoff; Comprone; Costanzo; Kligerman; D. Murray; Wiener). Long before the rise of digital audio technologies, compositionists have been exploring ways that speaking and writing interanimate one another—elucidating how auditory classroom activities can help students invent and revise their print writing (Corbett; Elbow; Moffett; Smitherman; Shor). Certainly, emerging digital technologies open up new possibilities for integrating multimodal activities into the writing classroom, but it is important to remember that composition has always already been a field that has sought to help students draw connections between writing, image making, speaking, and listening. Ultimately, by placing new technologies such as digital audio in dialogue with past multimodal approaches to teaching composition, I hope to encourage teachers to consider ways they can employ digital multimodal composing in order to meet many of the objectives they already pursue as writing instructors.

Finally, by looking back at the ways past compositionists both celebrated and feared the impending "death of print" in the electronic age, I hope to remind us to take a critical perspective about the potentially hyperbolic claims that contemporary scholars have been making about the multimodal revolution. In seeking to offer a critical perspective about the rhetoric of new technologies in the field, I am drawing on a substantial tradition of scholarship in the subfield of computers-and-writing (Banks; Baron; Johnson-Eilola; C. Selfe and Hawisher; C. Selfe, *Technology*; Selber; Sullivan and Porter). Resisting the rhetoric of "progress" that is often used to market new educational technologies, numerous computers-and-writing scholars have argued persuasively that we must remain vigilant about the ways new technologies can be employed to reinforce both problematic pedagogical practices (Eldred; Hawisher and Selfe; Selber) and material inequalities of race, class, gender, and disability (Banks; Dolmage; Kirtley; Grabill; Moran, "Access"; C. Selfe and Hawisher). Yet, at the same time, computers-and-writing scholars have also powerfully critiqued the tendency of some humanists to simplistically dismiss all digital forms of composing as *inherently* harmful for students' development of writing and critical thinking skills (Baron; C. Selfe, *Technology*; Yancey). Challenging the common tendency to position new technologies as *either* inherently beneficial *or* inherently detrimental for the teaching of writing, compositionists have increasingly come to argue that we need to "pay attention" (C. Selfe, *Technology*) to the complex and multivalent effects of technologies within particular literacy education contexts.

While there has already been a great deal of scholarship critically engaging the rhetoric of computer technologies in the field from the 1980s to the present, I seek to extend this conversation by interrogating the rhetorical choices that compositionists made in discussing the electronic or multimedia revolution at the turn of the 1970s. Looking back to a period before the rise of the personal computer, I closely analyze the complex ways that past compositionists responded to the new media technologies—the slide projectors, the super 8 cameras, the televisions, the photocopiers, the tape recorders—of their time. In particular, I critically interrogate the often-hyperbolic claims that 1960s and 1970s compositionists made about electronic media's ability either to transform or to destroy the teaching of writing, suggesting that this history can cause us to be wary of the rhetoric of "crisis" that often undergirds contemporary discussions of new media in our field.

In looking to the past in order to develop a critical perspective on contemporary technologies, I am inspired by the work of numerous composition and rhetoric scholars who have demonstrated how historical inquiry can complicate current discussions of digital media (Baca; Banks; Baron; Delagrange; Kalmbach; Haas; Rice). For example, Adam Banks has powerfully shown how recent analyses of the "digital divide" can be critiqued and extended by attending to the rich and complex history of how African Americans have long sought "transformative access" (45) to a wide range of technologies, including television, textiles, architecture, and the legal system. Similarly, Angela Haas has suggested that contemporary theories of hypertext can be reimagined by examining the complex social practice of associative linking in Native American wampum belts—arguing persuasively (along with Banks) that our field's tendency to fetishize "new" technologies problematically works to reinforce racist and colonialist narratives of progress. Although my historical work does not focus on the crucial intersections of race and technology that Banks and Haas elucidate, my project runs parallel to theirs in that I seek to interrogate the often-hyperbolic rhetorics of social transformation that accompanied the introduction of analog media technologies into our field.

Finally, I would like to note that my historical recovery work owes a debt to Dennis Baron's *A Better Pencil: Readers, Writers, and the Digital Revolution*. In this fascinating historical study, Baron critically revisits the often overexaggerated hopes and fears that accompanied the introduction of such once-new writing technologies as the pencil, the typewriter, and the word processor—cautioning us to be wary of overestimating the degree to which new computer technologies will either improve or impede learning. While Baron critically examines how past educators responded to new *alphabetic* writing technologies, I seek to extend his work by uncovering and critically analyzing the ways that past teachers responded to the development of new *multimedia* composing tools.

SAMPLING THE PAST: REMIX AS HISTORICAL METHODOLOGY

When composition historians sift through the libraries of our field, we too often tend to focus on critiquing and categorizing. We organize our past into chronological narratives of progress: from current-traditional, through the process movement, to the social turn and beyond. We carve up the field into distinct epistemological categories—expressivist, cognitive, social-epistemic—and then we argue about which of these theoretical "camps" is best. In other words, we adopt the standpoint of the critic who seeks to point out the limitations of past approaches—to advance the field by agonistically refuting what came before. Although this kind of critical mapping can productively cause us to question our basic assumptions about writing pedagogy, it can also limit our ability to make reflective and inventive use of the vast historical resources—the articles, the textbooks, the monographs, the workshop reports—lying dusty in our archives.

In this book, then, I seek to move beyond the standpoint of the critic: to resee our fields' history from the perspective of the remix artist. When the remixer enters the record store or video archive, she doesn't seek to evaluate or categorize. Whereas the critic might dismiss the entire oeuvre of the Bee Gees as hopelessly formulaic and naïve, the remixer would scour the Bee Gees' work looking for an intriguing moment—a beat, a phrase, a chorus—that she could recombine with more contemporary material to create a new song.[1] Whereas the critic would strive to sort art works into genres and periods, the remixer would seek to creatively recombine disparate materials—to make a new composition by juxtaposing samples from radically disparate artistic traditions and periods.

By adopting the associative logic of the remix as a historical storytelling strategy, I ultimately hope to challenge the binary theoretical taxonomies and linear progress narratives that have too often led us to forget useful elements of our past. In telling stories of the "progress" of our discipline, composition scholars have often divided the field up into expressivist, cognitive, and social approaches (Berlin; Faigley), inner- and outer-directed theories (Bizzell), process and post-process paradigms (Kent), to name but a few. Although these taxonomies have been quite useful heuristics for making sense of the ideological and epistemological differences among pedagogical theories in our field, we must remember that theoretical taxonomies inevitably oversimplify the complex theorizing of the scholarship they attempt to map. As Lisa Ede powerfully argues,

> the world of both theory and practice in composition is more complex—and more situated—than most taxonomies can allow for. Scholars need terms and taxonomies to help organize our thinking, but we would do well to develop some healthy suspicions of them, particularly when they are used primarily to establish hierarchies and to create opposing theoretical camps that suggest that teachers can and should enact "purified" theoretical positions. (96–97)

Indeed, when we begin to look closely at the work of many of the "canonical" figures of composition history, we can come to recognize that they often exceed or complicate the theoretical categories into which they have traditionally been placed. For example, despite the expressivist label that has been applied to Peter Elbow, his work on peer response has always acknowledged (at least to some extent) the social aspects of the writing process. Even though Janet Emig has been called a cognitivist because of the research methodology she employed, her advocacy of personal writing might put her as much in the expressivist camp. Ann Berthoff may have strongly critiqued the positivist epistemology of cognitive psychologists, but she nevertheless remained deeply interested in the workings of the human mind. If we wish to gain a more nuanced understanding of the development of composition theory as a field, we must ultimately work to move beyond rigid taxonomies that tend to overemphasize the differences between scholars.[2]

Seeking to complicate common ways of mapping the field, I focus in this book on tracing the *unexpected connections* among scholars who have been traditionally viewed as belonging to diametrically opposed camps. Rather than highlighting how Linda Flower and Ann Berthoff differed in their beliefs about research methodology, I emphasize how they both sought to demonstrate the crucial role that multisensory mental imagery plays in the alphabetic writing process. Rather than rehashing the ideological divisions between Donald Murray and Ira Shor, I focus attention on how they shared an interest in employing visual composing technologies to help students resee and reimagine the world. Rather than dwelling on the epistemological differences between Edward Corbett and Janet Emig, I highlight the ways each sought to draw connections between alphabetic writing and other forms of composing. By revealing these kinds of unexpected affinities among seemingly disparate scholars, I hope to demonstrate that multimodal approaches to writing pedagogy have transcended the theoretical "camps" that have traditionally divided us—that multimodality is a key part of the common disciplinary heritage that we all share.

In crafting this history, I ultimately seek not to advocate one pedagogical approach over another but rather to offer a pluralist vision of how we can engage multimodal composition. I offer this pluralist vision because I believe that we must draw upon all the available modes of composition practice and theory in order to teach students to compose in all the available modes of media. Although scholars such as James Berlin have argued that an acceptance of a social-epistemic rhetoric necessarily entails a rejection of expressivist and cognitive approaches, I assert that it is possible to accept a critical, social constructionist view of knowledge while still valuing and employing cognitive and expressivist theories and practices. In particular, I argue (pace Burke) that all composition pedagogies, including the social epistemic, offer a "terministic screen" that highlights and obscures aspects of the "scene" of multimodal composing. Thus, our goal should not be to choose one pedagogy over another, but rather to consider how we can recombine them—remix them—in ways that can enable us to develop a more nuanced and complex view of what it means to teach composition in the contemporary digital moment.

Although I have made an effort to sample my multimodal pedagogy from a wide range of compositionists, I also acknowledge that this history—like all histories—forgets at least as much as it remembers. In my search through the composition archives, I have perused much more material than what remains in this manuscript. Many intriguing moments ended up on the cutting-room floor as I began to focus on telling a story about how composition has a rich multimodal heritage that is worth reclaiming. As a composition teacher committed to multimodality, I have quite consciously chosen to remix our past in order "to invent an origin from which I would like to have emerged" (Hawk 262)—consciously focused my attention on highlighting those relatively fleeting moments in our past when compositionists seemed to embrace a multimodal vision of the field. Although I have certainly attempted to represent my historical sources as fairly and accurately as possible, I also recognize that my choices of what to include and what to exclude have inevitably been influenced by the rhetorical narrative that I have been seeking to craft.

Finally, I think it important to acknowledge that my historical vision has been both enabled and constrained by the diverse embodied standpoints (Haraway) from which I see the world. For example, the story I tell here has almost certainly been shaped by my privileged position as a white, middle-class male; by my current location in a public university with a primarily young, white, and class-privileged student body; by my experiences teaching and administrating in laptop classrooms and hardwired computer labs; by my identification as queer and bisexual; by my experiences as a young student who employed auditory strategies of knowing as a way to "compensate" for a learning disability; by my commitments to social justice, feminism, and pacifism . . . to name but a few of the lenses through which I see our past.

When I reflect about the embodied standpoints from which I view our history, I am reminded that the story I tell here of our field is but one of many possible narratives that could be told. I certainly hope that other compositionists will find my historical narrative to be useful, but I have no desire to make some kind of final or definitive statement about our disciplinary heritage. Rather, I hope to inspire readers to make their own historical remixes of our field—to join with me and others in the continual process of crafting a "usable past" (Harris) that can help us reimagine what it means to study and teach composition in the contemporary digital moment.

CHAPTER OVERVIEW

In an effort to resist the limiting effects of both binary taxonomies and linear progress narratives, I arrange my historical tale as a kind of *associative remix*. In each of the chapters, I revisit similar time periods (1960s through 1980s) with a new lens, seeking to highlight unexpected connections among diverse texts. In chapter 1, "Creative Translations: Reimagining the Process Movement (1971–84)," I focus especially on elucidating how compositionists have studied and taught alphabetic writing as a profoundly multimodal thinking process that shares affinities with visual and performing arts. In particular, I demonstrate that composition scholars have long recognized the crucial role of nonverbal mental imagery in the writing process (Berthoff; Flower and Hayes; Perl; Sommers). Furthermore, I recover the ways in which past composition scholars actively contributed to interdisciplinary research about creative processes across art forms (Berthoff; Emig; Flower and Hayes). At the contemporary moment when we compositionists are increasingly redefining ourselves as scholars and teachers of multimodal composing, I argue that it makes sense to reclaim our heritage as a field dedicated to contributing to—and learning from—interdisciplinary conversations about composing across modalities.

In chapter 2, "Composing Voices: Writing Pedagogy as Auditory Art (1965–87)," I elucidate the ways that expressivist, rhetorical, and critical teachers integrated auditory forms of composing into their pedagogies. In particular, I listen closely to how composition teachers have employed the concepts of voice (Elbow; Winchester), rhetoric (Corbett; Moffett), dialogue (Shor; Freire), and dialect (Smitherman) to develop pedagogies that enable students to interrogate critically the dynamic interrelation between the spoken and written word. At the current moment when digital audio technologies are once again causing compositionists to pay attention to issues of sound, I argue that it is important that we recover and learn from our heritage as a field dedicated to exploring the intersections between the alphabetic and the auditory.

While the first two chapters of this book focus on how compositionists have theorized and taught writing as a multimodal process, the final two chapters analyze the diverse ways that past composition teachers engaged the "new media" technologies of their day. In chapter 3, "The First Time Print Died: Revisiting Composition's Multimedia Turn (1967–74)," I explore how compositionists sought to adapt their pedagogies to the electronic era by engaging students in both analyzing and *producing* multimedia texts such as slideshows and collages. While some compositionists primarily viewed multimedia composing as way to help students learn conventional writing skills (Burnett and Thomason; Corbett; Wiener), others more radically argued that the electronic revolution necessitated a rethinking of the field's conventional privileging of linearity and originality in print texts (Kytle; Sparke and McKowen). In addition to considering ways that we might productively build upon these multimedia pedagogies, I also critique (with the value of hindsight) some of the limitations and contradictions of the arguments that past compositionists made about the new media of their day, suggesting that we should apply the same critical lens to the similar arguments we are making about the new media of our time.

In chapter 4, "Zooming Out: Notes toward a History of Cameras-and-Writing" (1971–84)," I work to recover compositionists' substantial heritage of integrating visual composing technologies into writing pedagogy—a heritage that predates the rise of the personal computer in the field. I begin by looking closely at how compositionists have employed exercises in photography (Kligerman; D. Murray) and filmmaking (Comprone; Costanzo; Williamson) in order to help deepen students' understanding of rhetorical concepts and composing processes. I then turn to uncovering the crucial role of video production in the development of critical pedagogy, focusing especially on how Ira Shor demonstrated ways that experience with video composing could heighten students' critical consciousness of the ideological implications of mass media. By analyzing both the successes and failures of past approaches to integrating cameras-and-writing, I ultimately seek to suggest ways that we can develop complex, critical pedagogies that attend closely to both the similarities *and* the differences between alphabetic and visual forms of composing.

In each of the four chapters (and in the final epilogue), I ultimately aim to place past composition theories in dialogue with contemporary pedagogical practices. To this end, I frequently pause my historical narrative to suggest specific ways that contemporary teachers might critically build upon past theories to design multimodal pedagogies that meet the needs of diverse, twenty-first-century students. In offering these pedagogical suggestions, I at times make reference to particular kinds of activities, assignments, or technologies that teachers might employ; however, it is important to note that I do *not* intend these pedagogical examples to be in any way prescriptive. Like Lisa Ede, I recognize that composition is a deeply and complexly situated field, and thus it is impossible ever to suggest an activity or an approach that could be effective in all the diverse contexts in which compositionists work. As a result, my goal in this book is simply to encourage teachers to recognize that our field's multimodal heritage can be a powerful inventive resource—to encourage teachers to look to the past (as well as to the future) as they work to design unique, multimodal pedagogies in their own local contexts.

Part One

Composition Has Always
Already Been Multimodal

1

Creative Translations: Reimagining the Process Movement (1971–84)

BEFORE I BEGAN EXPERIMENTING with multimodal composing, I found that considerations of "process" remained largely unconscious in my work as a writer and teacher. I might start a new project by freewriting or by talking to a friend, but I rarely paused to reflect about my own processes of invention. I might ask students to write reflections about the revisions they chose to make in their work, but I never made the study of composing processes a truly central part of my classes. Certainly, I was aware that process scholarship played a crucial role in helping "establish composition as a research field" (Harris, *A Teaching* 55), and I also recognized that the process movement had laid the foundation for many of the pedagogical practices (such as multiple drafts) that I took for granted. But, like many others, I also tended to think of "process" as a theoretical movement whose time had passed, and I focused most of my attention on engaging cultural studies methodologies that promised to move the field beyond the process paradigm.

When I started to compose multimodal texts, however, I suddenly found myself thinking about issues of *process* at almost every turn. When I composed my first animated Flash movie (about eight years ago), I couldn't help but intensively reflect about the strategies I was employing to invent and revise this radically multimodal text. Faced with the new composing challenge of combining spoken words, alphabetic text, images, and music, I found myself persistently engaging numerous process-oriented questions: Should I start by searching for images, by drawing a sketch, or by recording myself talking aloud? What did it mean to revise a text in which multiple layers (images, words, sounds) occurred simultaneously on a timeline? How much of my knowledge of alphabetic writing strategies could I transfer to these new modalities of composing? Was freewriting really a useful way to invent ideas for a Flash movie?[1]

In addition to wondering about how my traditional alphabetic invention strategies applied to multimodal composing, I also began to explore new invention strategies that I had never considered before. For example, I realized that digitally recording and editing my extemporaneous speaking was a useful strategy for developing the "voiceover narration" for my Flash movie; after that, I also began to use digitally recorded "free talking" as a way to invent ideas for alphabetic texts. In other words, I started to recognize that experimenting with multimodal composing could ultimately be a way for me to resee or reimagine the alphabetic writing process. In my teaching too, I began to make discussion of process a more conscious part of my pedagogy. I spent much time asking students to reflect critically about the similarities and differences in their processes of composing alphabetic and multimodal texts. We experimented with freewriting as a way to invent videos, and we explored visual storyboarding as a way to invent alphabetic essays. Ultimately, the collaborative investigation of composing processes started to become a central theme of my multimodal writing courses.

Seeking to contextualize these classroom explorations, I started to look back at the work of many of the foundational theorists of the process movement in the 1970s and 1980s (Berthoff; Emig; Flower and Hayes; Perl; Sommers). At first, I didn't expect that past process scholarship would be able to shed much light on the contemporary multimodal questions I had been asking; certainly, issues of multimodality were largely absent from all the histories of the process movement that I had read (Berlin; Crowley; Ede; Faigley; Foster; Harris; Henze, Selzer, and Sharer; Miller). Yet, when I began to re-read the work of 1970s and 1980s process theorists, I came to discover a rich tradition of compositionists studying and teaching writing in profoundly multimodal ways.

Challenging the common notion that the process movement was focused on words alone, I seek in this chapter to demonstrate ways that process researchers conceptualized alphabetic writing as a deeply multimodal thinking process that shares affinities with other forms of composing (visual, musical, spatial, gestural). In particular, I argue that process researchers engaged two interdisciplinary questions that remain highly relevant for multimodal compositionists today:

- Are there similarities in the creative composing processes of writers, visual artists, designers, and performing artists (Berthoff; Emig; Flower and Hayes)?
- What role do nonverbal modes of thinking play in the invention and revision of alphabetic texts (Berthoff; Flower and Hayes; Perl; Sommers)?

I recognize that I may seem a bit outdated in attempting to revive the 1970s and 1980s research of a group of scholars variously associated with the "process movement" in composition studies. Yet, as Lisa Ede has recently contended, the theorists of the process movement continue to influence contemporary pedagogical practice—even if many of their claims have been insightfully critiqued by "post-process" theorists.[2] After all, many of the core practices of writing teachers (multiple drafts, peer response, invention activities, contextual grammar instruction, formative feedback) continue to reveal the enduring influence of the process theories developed in the 1970s and early 1980s. Thus, as we begin to redefine the landscape of composition to incorporate digital multimodal production, it makes sense to return to these key theories to see how they might inform this shift.

To this end, I present in this chapter a series of three *tracks,* engaging oft-forgotten multimodal aspects of our field's process heritage. In track 1, "Creativity," I look closely at how Janet Emig positioned composition as an interdisciplinary field, calling for process scholars to gain new insights about writing by studying and practicing other arts. I then turn to Flower and Hayes's interdisciplinary investigation of writing and visual art as related creative problem-solving processes, considering how Flower and Hayes's research findings can inform contemporary digital multimodal composition pedagogy. I conclude by briefly elucidating how compositionists might productively reengage contemporary scholarship on creative cognition.

In track 2, "Translation," I look closely at process researchers' investigation of the role of nonverbal mental imagery in the invention and revision of alphabetic writing. In particular, I focus attention on Flower and Hayes's provocative definition of writing as an act of translation from the multimodal mind to the alphabetic page. I argue that Flower and Hayes's translation theory can provoke us to consider including multimodal invention activities in writing classes, and it can also propel us to question the limitations of alphabetic writing as a form of communication. In addition to analyzing the work of Flower and Hayes, I also briefly elucidate ways that Sondra Perl's exploration of felt sense and Nancy Sommers's discussion of revision can contribute to the study and teaching of composing as a multimodal thinking process.

In track 3, "Imagination," I turn to analyzing how Ann Berthoff theorized composing as a multimodal process of making meaning, urging composition teachers to help students draw connections between alphabetic writing and all the other forms of composing that they use to make sense of the world. Challenging the common notion that Berthoff's theory of the imagination was focused solely on the epistemic power of words, I argue that Berthoff ultimately sought to demonstrate ways that thought and reality are socially constructed through multiple symbol systems (alphabetic, musical, visual, gestural).

TRACK I: CREATIVITY

I begin this recovery project with Janet Emig's 1971 *Composing Processes of Twelfth Graders*—a text that has been widely recognized as foundational for the development of process approaches for researching and teaching composition. Although scholars have articulated Emig's great contribution to establishing compositionists' disciplinary expertise in the teaching of alphabetic writing (Berlin; Ede), historians have largely passed over the ways Emig's work both draws upon and contributes to *interdisciplinary* research on creative composing across modalities. In her 1971 study, Janet Emig defines composing very broadly as "the selection and ordering of elements" (66). When people are "composing in writing" (1), they are selecting and ordering words; when people are composing a painting or composing a symphony, they are selecting and ordering auditory or imagistic elements. Because Emig views composing as a concept that travels across modalities, she does not limit her literature review to research that focuses on alphabetic writing specifically. Rather, Emig seeks to position her study in relation to "research dealing with the whole or some part of what has been called, globally, the 'creative process'" (7). In discussing past global research on the creative process in visual art, writing, music, and science, Emig notes that "many students of creativity as well as creators across modes" (17) have proffered a view of the creative process as a sequence of stages. On the one hand, Emig argues that stage models of creativity (Cowley; Wallas; Wilson) are useful because they demonstrate that "there are elements, moments, and stages within the composing process which can be distinguished and characterized in some detail" (33). On the other hand, she questions the tendency of stage models to portray the creative process as a linear sequence—arguing instead that the various elements or stages of the composing process occur recursively. In this way, Emig proposes a revision of stage models of creativity (from linear to recursive) that could potentially apply well beyond the walls of the writing classroom or even of the English department.

Ultimately, Emig suggests that English teachers should not limit themselves to studying and teaching the composing of alphabetic texts alone—that English teachers have much to gain by studying and teaching other forms of composing. Indeed, Emig notes regretfully that very few teacher-training programs in the United States offer

> experiences in allied arts through creative arts workshops. When, if ever, have our secondary school teachers painted, sung, or sculpted under any academic auspices? Partially because they have no direct experience of composing, teachers of English err in important ways. They underconceptualize the process of composing. Planning degenerates into outlining; reformulating becomes the correction of minor infelicities. (98)

In addition to proffering the now common assertion that teachers of writing should themselves be writers (98), Emig also suggests more radically that teachers of writing should gain experience composing with a wide range of modalities. In particular, Emig argues that experience in composing across modalities (alphabetic, aural, visual, or spatial) can help teachers understand invention (planning) and revision (reformulating) as complex recursive processes, moving beyond teaching formulaic, product-centered models such as the "five paragraph theme" (97).

In this way, Emig outlines a truly radical vision of what it means to study and teach *composition*. Challenging the notion that compositionists should focus on alphabetic writing exclusively, Emig suggests that writing teachers should join with "allied arts" fields in the interdisciplinary study and practice of creative composing—in exploring the recursive, generative process of "selecting and ordering elements" (66) that is common across modalities. Compositionists seeking to gain insight into revision need not necessarily restrict their investigation to the processes of alphabetic writers; rather, compositionists might study how painters and sculptors revise ideas during the process of composing, considering how their visual revising strategies might be adapted to alphabetic writing.

Emig's call for compositionists to engage in the interdisciplinary study of creative composing gains even more relevance in the contemporary digital moment. Although Emig could assume that visual, aural, and alphabetic composing were separate though related activities, digital technologies increasingly enable students to compose texts that blend images, sounds, and words. In an environment where distinctions between alphabetic writing, art, design, and music are breaking down (Manovich; New London Group), it is important that we help students gain a global understanding of creative processes that is not tied to any specific modality—an understanding that they can use to help guide their composing with diverse alphabetic, audio, and visual materials.

Although Emig called for interdisciplinary collaboration in the study and teaching of composing across modalities, her *Composing Processes of Twelfth Graders* remains, after all, a single-authored text. In contrast, Linda Flower (a compositionist) and John Hayes (a cognitive psychologist) actually enacted interdisciplinary collaboration in their research on writing as a creative problem-solving process. When Flower and Hayes discuss problem solving, they are generally referring to a goal-directed activity that occurs whenever people find themselves "at some point 'A' and wish to be at another point 'B'; for example, when they have a new insight into Hamlet, but have yet to write the paper that will explain it" ("Cognition of Discovery" 22). Rejecting the notion that all problem solving is simplistic or rote, Flower and Hayes argue in a 1980 article that the writer's problem "is never merely a given: it is an elaborate construction which the writer creates in the act of composing. . . . Even though a teacher gives 20 students the same assignment, *the writers themselves create the problem they solve*" ("Cognition of Discovery" 22–23). During the recursive creative process of defining or finding the problem, the writer may spend extensive time analyzing the rhetorical situation (audience, exigency) as well as formulating goals (for affecting readers, for creating a persona, for conveying meanings).

Arguing that research on writers' problem finding can contribute to the development of a generalizable theory of creativity, Flower and Hayes assert that "if we can describe how a person represents his own problem in the act of writing, we will be describing a part of what makes a writer 'creative'" ("Cognition of Discovery" 30). In particular, Flower and Hayes seek to demonstrate that problem finding is a creative cognitive activity common to both alphabetic writing and fine art:

A recent long-range study of development of creative skill in fine art [Getzels and Csikszentmihalyi] showed some striking parallels between successful artists and our expert writers . . . In this experiment, the artists were given a studio equipped with materials and a collection of objects they might draw. The successful artists, like our expert writers, explored more of the materials before them and explored them in more depth, fingering, moving, touching, rearranging, and playing with alternatives, versus moving quickly to a rather conventional arrangement and sketch. Once drawing was begun, the artists' willingness to explore and reformulate the problem continued, often until the drawing was nearly completed. Similarly our successful writers continued to develop and alter their representation of the problem throughout the writing process. This important study of creativity in fine art suggested that problem-finding is a talent, a cognitive skill which can lead to creativity. The parallels between these two studies suggest that problem finding in both literature and art is related not only to success, but in some less well-defined way to 'creativity' itself. ("Cognition of Discovery" 30–31)

In this way, Flower and Hayes demonstrate that both alphabetic and visual creativity entail a willingness to intensively explore materials—to "rearrange" and "play with alternatives" (30–31). An artist drawing a still life (like the ones in the above experiment) will compose a more creative product if she takes the time to explore the many possible ways she might represent and rearrange a series of objects. Similarly, a writer composing a research-based essay would be well advised to consider a wide variety of sources on a topic, exploring ways he might creatively transform and combine those sources to develop a novel argument. As writers and artists engage in the composing process (as they transform and rearrange materials on paper, on screen, on canvas), they may often find themselves redefining their problems, generating new ideas and imagining new goals (Flower and Hayes, "Cognition of Discovery," 30–31).

By suggesting that problem finding is a generic process common to alphabetic writing and visual artistic production, Flower and Hayes implicitly challenge the common notion that alphabetic writing and the visual arts are entirely separate fields. Although English composition instructors and visual studio art instructors teach students to compose very different kinds of products, they share a concern with teaching students to engage in composing as a recursive process of discovery—a process in which composers continuously redefine their "problem" as they intensively explore, transform, and rearrange materials (words, images, objects). If students could be taught a common vocabulary for understanding the creative processes of composing words and composing images, they might better be able to transfer their skills in problem finding from one modality to another.

In seeking to develop common vocabularies for understanding visual and alphabetic composing, it could be useful for us to take up Emig, Flower, and Hayes's suggestion that we collaborate with scholars in "allied arts" fields in studying the creative process. Indeed, even though compositionists have largely avoided participating in the interdisciplinary study of creativity in the past twenty years, the interdisciplinary field of creative cognition has flourished (Gardner, *Art*; Martindale; Finke, Ward, and Smith) and has begun to be taken up by humanist scholars of literature, music, and the visual arts (Hogan; Turner).[3] For example, in a recent book, *Cognitive Science, Literature, and the Arts*, Patrick Colm Hogan draws on cognitive science research to explore similarities in the creative composing processes of famous artists, musicians, and literary writers. In particular, Hogan demonstrates ways that creative artists in a variety of modalities all tend to exhibit states of defocused attention—moments when they are able to move beyond proximate associations (the most obvious words, images, or sounds that come to mind) to explore remote associations (to connect words, images, or sounds that would normally seem disparate). Looking at the works of a variety of artists and writers, Hogan suggests that composers are better able to make remote associations if they draw upon and combine multiple creative traditions in composing their work (for example, taking inspiration for a play from the structure of a poem, blending African sculpture and contemporary Western art). Although scholars of creative cognition attempt to delineate elements of creative process that may be generalizable across art forms, they also have increasingly come to recognize that creativity necessitates domain-specific knowledge and that what counts as "creative" in a particular situation is at least in part socially constructed (Gardner, *Art*; Hogan).

Although I recognize the limitations of generalizable theories of creativity, I nevertheless suggest that it could be useful for compositionists to conduct comparative studies of students' creative processes when composing alphabetic and visual texts. While Emig and Flower and Hayes all used think-aloud methodologies to study creative process, we might instead employ the more contemporary methodology of video screen capture (Geisler and Slattery) to analyze the rhetorical choices that students make in composing visual and alphabetic texts. In a screen capture study, the researcher uses specialized software to record everything that happens on a participant's screen while he or she is composing. After closely analyzing and coding the video screen capture data, the researcher then conducts "stimulated recall interviews" (Geisler and Slattery 198) in which they show participants clips of the captured video and ask them to discuss the choices they made and the activities in which they engaged. By comparing interview and video-capture data of students composing with diverse modalities, we might better be able to articulate the similarities and differences in the ways students approach alphabetic and video composing tasks. Although these kinds of studies certainly could not account for all the complex social and ideological factors that influence composing, they nevertheless could help us develop some useful (though limited) heuristics for discussing process that could potentially transfer across the diverse modalities that students use to compose.

TRACK 2: TRANSLATION

In addition to demonstrating that alphabetic writing shares similarities to other forms of composing, Flower and Hayes also articulate how the act of alphabetic writing entails *multimodal thinking*—how writers do not think in words alone. In particular, Flower and Hayes focus attention on the powerful role of mental imagery in writers' thinking processes.[4] Describing the process of planning in which writers generate ideas, create rhetorical goals, and develop organizational schemes, Flower and Hayes assert in a 1981 article that "the information generated in planning may be represented in a variety of symbol systems, such as imagery or kinetic sensations" ("A Cognitive Process" 373). If writing about a remembered place, the writer might perceive sensory (auditory, visual, olfactory) images of that place. Instead of setting a rhetorical goal in words, the writer might picture an audience member and imagine how he or she would react to the writing. The writer might imagine the organization of the piece in terms of a visual shape rather than in terms of a verbal outline. Even when writers are planning verbally, they are not necessarily thinking in prose-like sentences; "a whole network of ideas might be represented by a single key word" ("A Cognitive Process" 373). Seeking to emphasize the fact that writers do not think in words alone, Flower and Hayes define the drafting of alphabetic text as an act of translation.[5] In the Flower and Hayes model, translating refers to

> the process of putting ideas into visible language. We have chosen the term translate for this process over other terms such as "transcribe" or "write" in order to emphasize the peculiar qualities of this task. . . . Trying to capture the movement of a deer on ice in language is clearly a kind of translation. Even when the planning process represents one's thoughts in words, that representation is unlikely to be in the elaborate syntax of written English. So the writer's task is to translate a meaning. ("A Cognitive Process" 373)

Although Flower and Hayes recognize that translating from multimodal internal representations to alphabetic external representations is a challenging activity, they also tend to assume that it is a given of the writing process—an unavoidable constraint. Responding to an alphabetic writing prompt in a time-limited laboratory setting, Flower and Hayes's research subjects were given neither the time nor the means to create external representations of knowledge in any medium but alphabetic text (or simple visual symbols such as arrows and circles).

Yet, when we move from the research lab of 1980s to the contemporary composition class of today, writers need not necessarily be constrained to producing only alphabetic external representations of knowledge. Many contemporary composition teachers (though certainly not all) can offer students both the time and the means to create external representations of knowledge in a variety of modalities. Rather than seeing translation as a reductive process of moving from multimodal mind to alphabetic page, we can instead reimagine translation as a dynamic process of moving between internal multimodal representations of knowledge (in the mind) and external multimodal representations (on the computer or the page).

At the very least, Flower and Hayes's theory suggests the value in having students complete multimodal activities as part of the process of planning alphabetic writing. If we restrict students to word-based planning activities (for generating ideas, for defining rhetorical purpose, for analyzing audience), we may be unduly limiting their ability to think deeply about their rhetorical tasks. For example, students might think about their audience in richly complex mental imagery, but have trouble defining their audience in words. If we give students the opportunity to create a visual representation of their audiences (using found images or original drawings), we may be able to gain a much richer sense of their rhetorical thinking than if we limited them to verbal audience analysis alone. Similarly, we might be able to help students to think beyond the five-paragraph essay if we let them imagine the organization of their writing in visual terms, creating a storyboard instead of a conventional outline. With Flower and Hayes's translation theory in mind, it is possible to imagine teaching writing as a multimodal thinking process not just an alphabetic product.

Although Flower and Hayes offer the most extended analysis of the role of multimodal thinking in the writing process, other process researchers (Perl; Sommers) also highlight the ways writers draw on nonverbal mental imagery in inventing and revising their work. For instance, Sondra Perl argues in her 1980 article "Understanding Composing" that writing researchers must pay attention to those aspects of the composing process that are "not so easy to document" because they "cannot immediately be identified with words" (364). Seeking to explain "what happens when writers pause and seem to listen to or otherwise react to what is inside of them" (365), Perl turns to the theory of *felt sense* outlined by the psychologist and philosopher Eugene Gendlin. Explaining the central role of multimodal felt sense in a writer's invention, Perl notes that "when writers are given a topic, the topic itself evokes a felt sense in them. This topic calls forth images, words, ideas, and vague fuzzy feelings.

. . . When writers pause, they are looking to felt experience, and waiting for an image, a word, or a phrase to emerge that captures the sense they embody" (365). In this way, Perl (like Flower and Hayes) suggests that writing is a kind of translation—a movement from the multimodal world of the mind (where images, words, and kinesthetic sensations mingle) to the alphabetic space of the page (where conventionally only words appear).

In contrast to Perl's emphasis on the role of multimodal thinking in invention, Nancy Sommers highlights the role of multimodal thinking in *revision*. In a classic 1980 study, "Revision Strategies of Student Writers and Experienced Adult Writers," Sommers notes that students tend to "understand the revision process as a rewording activity" (381). In focusing on deleting unnecessary words or choosing better words, students ultimately think of revision as an attempt to clean up the redundancy and imprecision of speech (381–83). In contrast, experienced writers move beyond an understanding of revision as rewording to a broader conception of revision as a process of reordering, adding to, and transforming ideas. In outlining this more global understanding of revision, experienced writers often talk in *visual-spatial* terms: "the experienced writers describe their primary objective when revising as finding the form or shape of their argument. Although the metaphors vary, the experienced writers often use structural expressions such as 'finding a framework,' 'a pattern,' or 'a design' for their argument" (Sommers 384). In this way, Sommers suggests that visual-spatial thinking (conceiving of writing as a shape or structure) can be a useful way of moving beyond rewording to considering more global changes of organization and argument. Although Sommers asserts that experienced writers' visual-spatial thinking is largely an internal mental process, it is possible to imagine course activities that might literalize the notion of conceptualizing writing as a shape or pattern. In order to get students past their habit of reading over their text looking for words to delete or change, we could ask students to translate their text into a spatial image—to create an external representation of their text that is not tied to words alone. By translating their texts into images, students might better be able to radically revise—radically *resee*—their alphabetic writing.

In addition to helping us consider ways that multimodal activities might enhance students' composing of alphabetic texts, process scholarship can also provocatively lead us to question the limitations of alphabetic writing as a modality of communication. In a lesser-known 1984 article, "Images, Plans, and Prose," Flower and Hayes assert that "as writers compose they create multiple representations of meaning. Some of these representations, such as an imagistic one, will be better at expressing certain kinds of meaning than prose would be, and some will be more difficult to translate into prose than others" (122). Questioning the notion that alphabetic text is always the best way to express ideas, Flower and Hayes demonstrate that "writers must often struggle to capture, in words, information that would better be expressed in other ways" ("Images" 132).

Providing an example of a rhetorical purpose that cannot be adequately met with words alone, Flower and Hayes offer a detailed discussion of field guides for bird identification:

> the text is clearly secondary to the pictures. And even then, the major guides—such as the Audubon, Golden, and Putnam Guides—are divided regarding which is better: a photograph that supplies a context or an artist's rendering that more clearly identifies details and color. . . . The limitations of prose become obvious, however, when these writers try to capture another critical feature of the bird—its song. You know you are in trouble with the whiskered owl when the text tells you that the "distinctive call, 4 to 9 high pitched *boos* slowing at the end, is the best means of identification." . . . Robbins et al. (1966), in fact, try to supplement words with the visual representation of a sonogram: an inch-long graph with squiggles, dots and smudged bars. Any port in a storm. ("Images" 132)

In sharing this tale of the incredible challenge of representing bird song in print, Flower and Hayes ultimately suggest that alphabetic text is not necessarily the best modality for representing all kinds of knowledge. Although in 1984 (when Flower and Hayes published their article) there was no clear alternative to print-based field guides, bird-watchers today can purchase an "iBird explorer" application for their iPhone that provides ready access to images and sound samples of large quantities of birds ("iBird"). In this way, we can see that contemporary portable digital technologies increasingly offer composers more ways of expressing knowledge when alphabetic text falters.

Although it may not be very common for composition students to struggle to represent birdsongs in their writing, it is much more common for students to struggle to write analytically about pieces of music. Certainly, students can easily translate lyrics to alphabetic text, but it is much harder to translate pitch, rhythm, tone, and so forth. In order to help an audience follow their analysis of a musical piece, students might compose a digital audio file instead of an alphabetic paper—interspersing audio samples from the piece of music with their own spoken commentary. By providing students with the option to compose using media other than print, we may greatly proliferate the kinds of ideas they can express in their analytical work.

Ultimately, if some information might "better be expressed in other ways" than words ("Images" 132), it makes sense to reimagine composition as a course that teaches students to discover—to choose—the modalities that best help them convey what they want to communicate. Instead of requiring students to move directly from multimodal mind to alphabetic page, we could instead teach students to translate ideas about a topic in multiple ways: gathering or creating visual images, drafting words, recording speech, gathering or creating music and atmospheric sounds. Once students have created a variety of external representations of knowledge in a variety of modalities, we could then ask them to consider which modalities would best help them achieve their rhetorical goals: Could they easily translate their images and sounds into alphabetic text or would too much be lost? Could their images stand alone without words to explain them? Should they consider combining words, images, and sounds using multimedia software (PowerPoint, Movie Maker, iMovie)? Which modalities would be most persuasive to their particular audience? Which modalities would enable them to create the persona they are attempting to achieve? Rather than requiring that students pursue the act of translation with the ultimate goal of producing an alphabetic text, we could instead teach students to engage in multi-modal translation with the ultimate goal of being able to make an informed rhetorical choice about which modalities best enable them to persuasively present their thoughts to a specific audience.

TRACK 3: IMAGINATION

Although Ann Berthoff is most often remembered for being highly critical of the positivist presuppositions of cognitive psychologists (Berlin, *Rhetoric*), it is important to note that she shared Flower and Hayes's belief that the mental process of composing was a profoundly multimodal activity. Whereas Flower and Hayes arrived at this conclusion through empirical research and cognitive psychological theory, Berthoff drew much of her belief about the multimodality of the mind from such humanistic thinkers as Coleridge, Langer, and Cassirer.[6]

Seeking to offer a robust metaphor for the ways people make meaning through multiple symbol systems, Berthoff turns to Coleridge's theory of the imagination as "the living power and prime agent of all human perception" (Coleridge, qtd. in Berthoff, *The Making* 28). By reclaiming the imagination, Berthoff ultimately seeks to highlight the ways that all sensory perception is mediated—the ways that sensory perception is always already a process of making meaning:

> The imagination is the shaping power: perception works by forming—finding forms, creating forms, recognizing forms, interpreting forms. Let me read you what Rudolph Arnheim, in his superb book *Visual Thinking,* lists as the operations involved in perception: active exploration, selection, grasping of essentials, simplification, abstraction, analysis and synthesis, completion, correction, comparison, problem-solving, as well as combining, separating, putting in context." Doesn't that sound like an excellent course in writing? To think of perception as *visual thinking* helps make the case for observation in the composition classroom, not for the sake of manufacturing "specifics" and vivid detail about nothing much, but because perception is the mind in action. (*The Making* 64)

Challenging the notion that sight gives us direct access to reality, Berthoff points out that visual perception is itself a form of composing. As we look at the world and compose visual images in our minds, we are constantly making meaning by selecting, arranging, and classifying—participating in an ultimately social process in which we construe what we see in relation to what we have seen in the past and what we *expect* to see in a given context (*Forming* 32). In this way, Berthoff argues that visual mental imagery is not just "source material" for writing (as Flower and Hayes suggest); rather, Berthoff shows that the process of composing mental images—the process of visual thinking—is analogous to writing. If we can teach students to understand how they make meaning with visual imagery in their minds, we may be able also to help them develop a more critical consciousness of how they make meaning on the page.

Further drawing connections between alphabetic writing and other forms of composing, Berthoff asserts that composition students and teachers might best be able to understand writing as an imaginative process by studying the work of visual and performing artists who make (or form) meaning with images, sounds, movements, and tactile objects: "Artists at work have a lot to teach us about the composing process. I think there is probably more to be learned by teachers of writing from time spent backstage and in practice rooms and studios than from time spent at conferences or in the study of rhetorical theory. We need to see the imagination in action in order to understand it as the forming power" (*Reclaiming* 261). In this way, Berthoff argues that there are commonalties between the composing processes of writers, visual artists, and performers—that there is much to be learned about the teaching of writing through the study of related arts. Challenging the notion that English teachers should confine themselves to studying the imaginative process of composing with words, Berthoff radically suggests instead that English teachers turn their attention to the study of the diverse ways that people make meaning of the world using multiple symbol systems:

> From craftsmen we can learn something about the relation-
> ship of pattern and design to forming; from artists we can

learn even more fundamental truths about forming–that you don't begin at the beginning, that intention and structure are dialectically related, that the search for limits is itself heuristic, that form emerges from chaos, that you say in order to discover what you mean, that you invent in order to understand and so on. (*The Making* 103–4).

Just as writers discover their meaning in the process of writing, so too do sculptors discover their ideas in the process of molding clay. Just as painters have learned to value the importance of generating chaos, so too must writers come to recognize that it is often unnecessarily constraining to begin with a rigid outline before composing has started. Just as musicians recognize the inventive possibilities of imposing a structure or limit on their arrangement of notes, so too may writers find that the search for limits, the search for structure, can themselves be methods of invention.

In seeking to teach students to understand writing as a "nonlinear, dialectical process" of making meaning (*The Making* 3), Berthoff ultimately suggests that "anything we can do to make composing not entirely different from anything else our students have ever done will be helpful" (*The Making* 10). In Berthoff's view, teachers should build upon the knowledge of composing that students already bring with them to the classroom. If a student, for example, has already come to appreciate the fact that she could generate ideas through the process of sculpting, then that student might be encouraged to transfer her understanding of sculpting as a process of discovery to considering writing as a process of discovery. By focusing the teaching of composition on harnessing the "active mind" of the student rather on evaluating the formal correctness of alphabetic products, Berthoff ultimately seeks to develop a composition pedagogy that could enable students to draw connections among—and develop a vocabulary for—all the varied ways they make meaning in their lives.

Berthoff's call for a composition pedagogy that helps students draw connections between writing and other arts gains renewed relevance in the contemporary digital moment. As composing technologies proliferate, many students (though certainly not all) are arriving in our classrooms with experience crafting a wide variety of texts beyond the printed, alphabetic essay: still images, videos, electronic music, blog entries to name but a few (C. Selfe and Hawisher; Yancey). Rather than implicitly suggesting to students that all of their out-of-school composing in multiple modalities is irrelevant to the work of the writing class, we might instead follow Berthoff in considering ways to help students draw connections among the many diverse kinds of composing experiences they have had in the past and will have in the future.

Revealing her persistent interest in helping students draw connections between visual and alphabetic composing, Berthoff includes several visual production activities in her textbook *Forming, Thinking, Writing: The Composing Imagination.* For example, Berthoff encourages students both to write and to visually sketch observations of a common object over a week's time (14). She then asks students to "observe their observations"—to explore how both their written descriptions and their visual sketches entail an active process of making meaning. Whether they are writing words or drawing visual images, Berthoff ultimately wants students to pause and reflect about how observation is an active, constructive process. Further engaging students in exploring the ways that visual images construct reality, Berthoff offers an assignment in which students design two versions of a poster for a political speech on campus: one that subtly supports the message of the speech and one that subtly critiques it (*Forming* 133). In this way, Berthoff implicitly argues that the composition class is about more than the writing of alphabetic text. For Berthoff, the composition class is ultimately a place where students employ multiple symbol systems (alphabetic, visual, auditory) in order to observe their observations and interpret their interpretations.

Although I believe that Berthoff's work offers a useful theoretical framework for integrating multimodal composing into writing classes, I must concede that her textbook, *Forming, Thinking, Writing,* includes relatively few visual production activities, keeping the focus largely on the composing of alphabetic text. Yet, when we look at the writings that Berthoff urges composition teachers to read, we can see glimpses of a more radical vision of composing across the curriculum—a vision that would engage students in employing multiple symbol systems to form concepts. For example, in her collection *The Making of Meaning,* Berthoff includes an excerpted article from the magazine of the Teachers' and Writers' Collaborative (TWC)—a group that seeks to integrate writing and visual arts instruction in New York City schools. Berthoff praises the TWC for their innovative work of placing

> poets and painters in the classroom with the aim of encouraging students in drawing and carving, building and constructing—making meaning all the way. Transformation is the generative idea: dreams become stories; stories become plays; drawings become puppets; observations become notes, which become biographies, reports, meditations. This kind of change will always make meaning because the active mind is engaged in asking what's happening? What am I doing? What do you think? How would I know? (*The Making* 197)

In this way, Berthoff radically asserts that transforming the representation of a concept from one medium or modality to another—from drawing to report, from puppet to play—can ultimately be a way to engage students in actively reflecting on the processes through which they make meaning of the world. In Berthoff's view, students may gain a richer understanding of a concept if they attempt to form that concept using multiple symbol systems; indeed, attempting to form a concept with multiple symbol systems may ultimately be a way to generate the chaos that leads to creative invention.

In addition to recommending the work of the TWC as a model in general, Berthoff especially suggests that teachers pay attention to the implications of Bob Sievert's "Basic Bug" project that was sponsored by the TWC. In this project, third- and fourth-grade students individually composed images and words about their personal experiences of insects, then collaboratively worked to develop diagrams and models of a "basic bug" that included many features common to insects, and then finally worked to represent their new knowledge of insects by collaboratively making murals and 8mm films. In explaining why she included Sievert's work in a collection for teachers of writing at all levels, Berthoff argues that Sievert offers a very useful understanding of the social process of concept formation, noting that "if I had to choose between chapter 5 of Vygotsky's *Thought and Language* and Bob Sievert's 'Bugs: One Insect Leads to Another' as a text to explain concept formation, I would take Sievert" (*The Making* 198). By pointing to Sievert's multimodal bug project as essential reading for any teacher at any level who seeks to help students form concepts, Berthoff implicitly argues for a reconsideration of the exclusive focus on alphabetic text in the academy—suggesting that students might develop a richer understanding of course concepts if they were able to compose about them using multiple modalities.

Of course, it can be argued that Sievert's multimodal bug project is irrelevant to college teaching because Sievert focuses on the elementary classroom. Yet, Berthoff repeatedly urges college teachers to resist their tendency to dismiss the insights of elementary instructors. For example, in the introduction to *The Making of Meaning*, Berthoff writes that she subscribes "wholeheartedly to Sylvia Ashton-Warner's notion that the end of 'the education story' can't be told unless we know the beginning. . . . Just as metaphor provides a focus for the study of meaning, so, I think considering how children learn is the best way to learn how to teach writing [in college] as a process of forming" (*The Making* vi). In the same volume, Berthoff underscores this point by perhaps hyperbolically suggesting that all candidates for the PhD in rhetoric "be required to teach third grade for a year" (23).

In other words, although professors might not be able to import Sievert's practices directly to the college classroom, they would be well advised to consider his insight that the forming of concepts is a richly multimodal process and that the separation of writing from visual art is a hindrance to students' learning. If we take Sievert's theories of learning seriously (as Berthoff asks us to do), we might begin to reimagine writing-across-the-curriculum programs as composing-across-the-curriculum programs—exploring, for example, ways that students might better learn scientific concepts if they both wrote about them and made videos about them.[7] Ultimately, if we looked closely at the elementary classroom (a space where numerous composing modalities are often taught in tandem), we might begin to question the disciplinary organization of the university that tends to separate the teaching of alphabetic writing from the teaching of other arts.

TRACK 4: REPRISE

In the past three tracks, I have sought to demonstrate that compositionists have a substantial history of studying and teaching multimodal composing—a history that predates the rise of the personal computer or the arrival of the graphical web. In telling this historical narrative, I ultimately hope to contribute to the project of constructing a "usable past" (Harris) that can productively inform the contemporary multimodal turn in composition studies. To this end, I offer here three refrains—three macrotheoretical principles—that can potentially help us reimagine what it means to study and teach composing in the contemporary digital moment.

Refrain 1: Alphabetic Writing Is a Profoundly Multimodal Process

Even when we are composing a solely alphabetic product, we often are thinking with multiple symbol systems (visual, auditory, gestural). As a result, multimodal composing activities can be a powerful way to help students invent ideas for and consider revisions of their alphabetic texts. If we limit students to only alphabetic means of invention and revision, we may unnecessarily constrain their ability to think intensively and complexly about their work. As a result, I suggest that composition teachers consider including one informal, multimodal composing activity as part of every major unit or sequence in their course.

As one multimodal way to help students begin to generate ideas for writing, teachers can engage students in imagistic "freecomposing." In this activity, students are asked to spend fifteen minutes or so searching online for images that associatively resonate with their current understanding of their topic (drawing on resources such as Flickr.com and Google image search). Just as in alphabetic freewriting, the goal is to quickly generate a wide variety of material without pausing to critically judge or evaluate. Once students have gathered a good number of images, they can then review their collection and select the three images that they find most compelling or intriguing. Ideally, students would then post their three selected images to a course blog (or discussion board) along with a written reflection discussing why they selected the images they did.

Because this process of associative imagistic invention may be new for students, teachers may wish to offer students some generative questions to guide their search process:

> What keywords come to mind when you think about this
> writing assignment?
> What images can you find when you use these keywords as
> search terms?
> Which of these images most resonate with your understand-
> ing of this topic? Why?
> Which images surprise you? Why?
> Who do you imagine as your audience for this project?
> Can you find images that represent that audience?

Furthermore, if students are having trouble finding images that are relevant, teachers could also invite them to draw a pen-and-paper sketch that represents the images that come to mind about their topic. For some students (especially those with a personal interest in drawing), the act of paper-based sketching may be a particularly conducive way to translate their imagistic thinking to the page (Dunn 65–82).

In addition to engaging in imagistic freecomposing, students also might be asked to create multimodal "cluster maps" using free online software such as Prezi.com. Whereas traditional cluster maps are limited to words and simple shapes such as lines and circles, Prezi can enable students to make a cluster map that combines words with embedded images and videos. In the process of making their cluster maps, students might search Google, YouTube, and library databases looking for quotations, images, and videos that relate to their chosen topic. They can then import all of this material into Prezi and experiment with multiple ways of arranging it. After students have created a Prezi map of their paper, they can then present their multimodal maps to each other, reflecting about how their understanding of their topic has changed through the process of gathering and rearranging their multimodal materials. By experimenting with diverse ways of arranging multimedia materials related to their topic, students can potentially develop lines of inquiry (and ultimately analytical claims) that they might not have discovered if they had been limited to alphabetic invention activities alone.

Although I think that multimodal invention activities have a crucial role to play in composition classrooms, I certainly do not mean to suggest that we turn away from more conventional alphabetic methods such as traditional freewriting, reading-response journals, descriptive outlines, annotated bibliographies, and paper-based cluster mapping. In my experience, some students will find imagistic composing activities particularly generative while others may find them less helpful; furthermore, some writing tasks may lend themselves to imagistic invention activities more than others. Rather than teaching students one standard set of methods for invention, then, we should instead introduce students to a wide range of visual and alphabetic strategies for generating ideas—engaging them in reflection about which techniques they find most useful and why.

Refrain 2: We Should Recognize the Limitations of Alphabetic Text as a Modality

Although alphabetic text is a powerful modality of communication, it cannot adequately convey all of the ideas composers might wish to express; at times, a writer may struggle to express in alphabetic words an idea that might better be expressed in another modality or combination of modalities (Flower and Hayes, "Images"; Kress). In order to help students learn to become rhetorically effective composers, it is essential that we teach them to consider critically which modality (alphabetic, visual, or aural) or combination of modalities will best enable them to convey their persuasive message.

As a way to help students begin to explore the unique affordances and limitations of different modalities, we might engage them in actively attempting to transform an argument from one modality to another. For example, students might attempt to "translate" the key argument of one of their alphabetic essays into a multimedia slideshow that combines still images and spoken voiceover (using iMovie on a Mac or Movie Maker on a PC). As students attempt to select and arrange images, spoken words, and titles to convey their argument, we can then prompt them to write a reflection considering questions such as:

- What aspects of your argument were easier to convey with images than words? Which aspects of your argument were harder to convey with words? Why?
- How did you need to revise your academic writing for spoken delivery?
- Why did you arrange and time your spoken words and images in the way you did? How did your arrangement of this video slideshow differ from your arrangement of your alphabetic text?
- How did your argument change when you attempted to transform it from an alphabetic paper to a video slideshow? How did your choice of modalities influence the kinds of ethical, pathetic, and logical appeals you were able to make?

By reflecting about the experience of attempting to make a similar argument using a variety of differing modalities, students can potentially develop a more nuanced understanding of the unique affordances of visual, aural, and alphabetic forms of communication.

In addition to asking students to experiment with transforming an argument from one modality to another, we also might offer students more open-ended assignments in which they must actively choose which modalities, genres, and technologies they will employ in order to convey an argument (Shipka "A Multimodal"). Because this kind of open-ended prompt can be challenging for students, it is essential that teachers engage students in a series of scaffolded, reflective activities to help them carefully articulate their rhetorical goals, analyze their audiences, and interrogate the unique affordances of diverse forms of media. As Jody Shipka notes, asking students to produce an account of their goals and choices [for an open-ended multimodal task] reminds them of the importance of *assessing rhetorical contexts, setting goals,* and *making purposeful choices.* More important, requiring students to produce these statements underscores the importance of being able to speak to goals and choices in a way that highlights *how, when, why,* and *for whom* those goals and choices afford and constrain different potentials for knowing, acting, and interacting. (Shipka, "A Multimodal" 288)

By engaging students in actively making and justifying choices about which modalities, technologies, and genres will best help them achieve their rhetorical goals, we can potentially help them develop a richer understanding of how rhetorical concepts such as audience, context, and exigency can be applied and adapted to diverse forms of composing.

Refrain 3: We Can Learn about Writing through Studying and Practicing Other Arts

As a field, we have a rich history of investigating connections between alphabetic writing and other forms of composing. Although there certainly are differences among various arts, it may be possible to develop theories of creative process that are at least partially transferable across modalities. Rather than teaching students to see alphabetic writing as entirely separate from all other forms of composing, we might instead engage students in collaboratively investigating the interrelation of alphabetic writing and other arts.

Following the example of Berthoff, we can begin by asking students to read essays about creative processes in various art forms as well as to write reflections about their own experiences composing with differing modalities. In many cases, students already come to our courses with some previous experience with nonalphabetic forms of communication (for example, taking a drawing class, shooting digital images, writing songs, making YouTube videos), but they tend to see these multimodal composing activities as wholly unrelated to the work of the writing class. By specifically asking students to write reflectively about their creative process across modalities, we can encourage them to begin to develop a transferable understanding of composing process that they can potentially apply to all the diverse forms of communication they are likely to employ in their lives.

In addition to asking students to reflect about their past multimodal composing experiences, it also can be useful to actually engage students in crafting a multimodal text as part of the work of the writing class. Depending on their particular curricular goals and technological resources, teachers might assign students to compose an audio essay, a video, a multimedia presentation, or a collage—to name but a few options.[8] Although these kinds of digital, multimodal projects will require different technical skills than alphabetic writing, we can nevertheless help students begin to develop a common language for analyzing both their alphabetic and their multimodal work. Whether we are asking students to compose an alphabetic text, a visual text, an audio text, or a text that combines modalities, we can engage them in reflective writing and oral discussion about such potentially transferable questions as:

- What is my goal or purpose for this text? How do I want people to think or act differently after they encounter it?
- Who is my audience for this text and how will I compose it with this audience in mind? What enthymematic assumptions does my audience have about the world?
- What strategies can I use to invent ideas for composing this text? What invention strategies seem to work best for me as a composer?
- How can I select and arrange the elements of this text (words, images, and sounds) in order to make them clear and persuasive to my audience?
- What strategies can I use to help me revise this text? What revision strategies seem to work best for me as a composer?

By organizing our courses around concerns of rhetoric and process that can potentially apply across modalities, we may be able to help students develop transferable composing skills. For example, a student who comes to understand the importance of audience when composing a video text may be able to transfer this understanding of audience to her composing of alphabetic texts; or, conversely, a student who develops an understanding of the importance of revision in alphabetic writing may then also come to recognize the power of revision in digital audio composing.

As we compositionists work to engage students in drawing connections among diverse forms of visual, auditory, and alphabetic composing, we must of course remember that we are not the only people in the university who have a stake in this project. Scholars of graphic design have substantial experience teaching students to compose visual texts for persuasive (and aesthetic) purposes. Scholars of music have a rich heritage of analyzing the social and cognitive processes involved in composing sounds. Scholars of film and video have developed a complex critical vocabulary for teaching students to analyze and to produce cinematic texts that blend visual, aural, and alphabetic modalities of communication. We clearly have much to learn from allied arts fields about the teaching of composing processes across modalities.

Unfortunately, however, the current disciplinary structure of the university tends to discourage both teachers and students from drawing connections among diverse composing arts. Too often, when a student moves from a design class, to a film class, to a music class, to a writing class, the student is likely to find that the teachers of those courses employ very distinct vocabularies to describe the creative process—vocabularies that appear to be relevant only to the particular modalities of composing on which the class centers. In order to counter this trend, we might consider working with colleagues in allied arts fields to develop interdisciplinary courses and programs that engage students in exploring the similarities and differences in various modalities of communication. Of course, I recognize that such interdisciplinary course and program development is devilishly difficult and may not be possible in all institutional contexts. Yet, even if we are unable to craft formalized interdisciplinary ventures, I would suggest that it is still worth making the effort to talk with (and read the scholarship of) our colleagues in allied arts fields—to consider ways we might redesign our pedagogies to help students draw connections between the interrelated fields of composition, music, film, and design.

2

Composing Voices: Writing Pedagogy as Auditory Art (1965–87)

WHEN I REFLECT ABOUT MY LIFE as a writer and teacher of composition, I don't just see printed pages: I hear voices speaking . . . I feel bodies moving.

I hear my third-grade teacher reading a poem I wrote aloud—breathing life into my words. Making me realize, for the first time, that the written word has power.

I feel the rush of joy I experienced the first time I performed on stage for an audience—the first time I set out to make an audience laugh and succeeded. At that moment, in the fifth grade, my lifelong fascination with rhetoric was born.

I hear myself alone in my room at age twelve, working on a play about environmental justice. I pace around the room talking to myself, then I stop and type at the Commodore 64, and then I pace and talk again. I feel the joy of creation . . . the passion for social change.

I hear myself working as a peer tutor, talking with a student about a very rough, sprawling draft. After about a half hour of conversation, the student speaks aloud a very clear outline of her argument. At that moment, I decide that I want to dedicate myself to teaching writing as a profession.

I hear the many conversations that have inspired this book—the many words spoken by students, colleagues, mentors, and friends that have found their way (often unconsciously) into my prose here.

I hear the rush of spoken words that have permeated my life as a writing teacher: the student conferences, the class discussions, the small group work, the minilectures, the hallway conversations.

Certainly, I will admit that I may be unusual in the degree to which I have drawn upon speaking and performing in my development as a writer and teacher; for example, my personal practice of pacing and talking aloud while writing is (I suspect) quite idiosyncratic. But, I would nevertheless suggest that most writers draw upon auditory forms of communication in their work at least some of the time. I would imagine that most readers of this volume can remember a conversation in which they (re)invented an idea for an alphabetic text. I would imagine that most readers of this volume can point to a spoken teaching moment (a conversation with a student, a class discussion) that they will remember for the rest of their lives. When we pause to listen for the sounds of composition, we can be reminded that alphabetic and aural communication are deeply intertwined— that the teaching of writing must necessarily be an auditory art.

Within the institutional structures of the contemporary U.S. academy, however, it often can be challenging for teachers to hear the auditory dimensions of composition pedagogy. Following the split between teachers of English and teachers of speech in 1914, we have increasingly seen a division between courses in composition taught in English or writing departments and courses in speech taught in communication departments (Mountford 409). Because composition courses are explicitly defined as focusing on writing and not speech, teachers of composition tend to deemphasize the relevance of the auditory elements of their classes—placing almost all of the evaluative weight on the alphabetic products that students write rather than on the spoken words that they say. When we privilege print forms of knowing above all else, we tend to delete from consciousness the myriad ways we draw upon auditory modalities of communication in our work as composition teachers and scholars.

Challenging the artificial bifurcation between the teaching of writing and the teaching of speaking, I seek in this chapter to demonstrate the crucial role that auditory forms of communication have played in the disciplinary development of composition as a field. Relistening to expressivist, rhetorical, and critical composition pedagogies from the 1960s, 1970s, and 1980s, I ultimately attempt to recover the voices of many compositionists who sought to:

- articulate the interconnections among alphabetic writing, speaking, reading, and listening (Corbett; Elbow; Moffett; Shor; Smitherman; Winchester);
- demonstrate the ways that auditory forms of composing can enhance the invention and revision of alphabetic texts (Corbett; Elbow; Moffett; Winchester);
- question the hegemony of print writing in composition, arguing for the importance of valuing auditory forms of knowing (Freire; Shor; Smitherman).

At the current moment, when compositionists are increasingly considering ways to integrate digital audio technologies into our work, it is vital that we recover our heritage as a field dedicated to helping students draw connections between the alphabetic and the auditory.

To this end, I offer here four tracks sampled from the 1960s, 1970s, and 1980s that turn up the volume on the aural aspects of composition pedagogy. In track 1, "Voice," I listen closely to Peter Elbow's and Otis Winchester's discussions of voice, focusing especially on the moments when they attend to voice as audible, embodied sound rather than as a metaphor of authenticity. In particular, I argue that Elbow and Winchester offer multimodal pedagogies that integrate writing, speaking, listening, and reading. Seeking to explore ways that expressivist voice pedagogies may be extended to address concerns of embodied difference, I conclude the track by placing Elbow's and Winchester's work in dialogue with Krista Ratcliffe's more recent feminist articulation of rhetorical listening.

In track 2, "Rhetoric," I revisit Edward P. J. Corbett's attempts to develop a classical rhetorical pedagogy that integrated the teaching of writing, speaking, and (to some extent) acting. In particular, I suggest that we take heed of Corbett's insight that experience with spoken performance can be a particularly useful way to develop students' understanding of audience analysis and ethos construction. Further elucidating the connections between spoken performance and rhetorical instruction, I turn to analyzing James Moffett's discussion of the role of dramatics in teaching students to understand and employ rhetorical concepts.

In track 3, "Dialogue," I analyze the auditory dimensions of the early critical pedagogy of Paulo Freire and Ira Shor. Highlighting the crucial role of spoken dialogue in the development of critical consciousness, I argue that critical teachers must come to question and ultimately resist the conventional privileging of alphabetic ways of knowing in the academy. Listening closely to Shor and Freire's discussions of the power of "talking books" and "collaborative oral dictation," I suggest ways that critical teachers can employ digital audio technologies in order to help students analyze and challenge unjust power structures.

In track 4, "Dialect," I engage Geneva Smitherman's 1970s scholarship on African American language practices and the politics of the teaching of English. In particular, I suggest that Smitherman's work can contribute to the ongoing development of multimodal pedagogy by 1) demonstrating the importance of valuing all the spoken and written dialects that students bring to the classroom; 2) challenging the conventional hegemony of print forms of knowledge in the university; 3) outlining a rhetorical approach for integrating the teaching of speaking, reading, writing, and listening in the composition classroom.

TRACK I: VOICE

In her recent history of aurality in writing instruction, Cynthia Selfe critically analyzes the "silence of voice" in composition studies ("Movement" 630). In Selfe's view, theorists of voice in composition have largely ignored the "embodied, physical human voice" in favor of the use of "metaphorical language that remediated voice as a characteristic of written prose" ("Movement" 630). In this way, Selfe asserts that voice theories have actually worked to reinforce the privileging of print modes of knowing in composition—to turn our attention away from the role of the embodied speaking voice in the act of composing. Although I see merit in Selfe's critique, I worry that she somewhat overstates the "silence" of voice in our field. Questioning Selfe's assertion that compositionists have historically focused solely on employing voice as a metaphor for alphabetic writing, I seek in this track to highlight ways that 1970s voice theorists productively sought to help students draw connections among the interrelated arts of speaking, writing, listening, and reading.

In recovering the auditory dimensions of voice pedagogy, I turn first to the foundational work of Peter Elbow. Although Elbow often uses voice as a metaphor to describe authenticity and power in words, he also emphatically argues that we must never forget that voice ultimately denotes material, embodied sounds—that "voice is produced by the body" ("What Do We Mean" 3). Elbow argues that although alphabetic texts are literally silent, "most readers experience some text as giving off more sense of sound—more of the illusion as we read that we are hearing the words. . . . when most people encounter a text—a set of words that just sit there silently on the page with no intonation, rhythm, accent, and so forth—they automatically project aurally some speech sounds into the text" ("What Do We Mean" 6–7).[1] Although I question the implicit assumption that speech is somehow more natural than writing, I have to admit that Elbow's voice resonates. For me, reading has always been a profoundly auditory activity. (Even when reading "silently," I really do hear the words on the page—so much so that I sometimes hear what sounds right and not what is actually visually there). Ultimately, Elbow's audible voice theory helps us understand that words are richly multimodal; they are both sounds and alphabetic signs. How we speak intertwines with how we write; how we listen intertwines with how we read. Writing is at least in part an auditory technology—a way of recording and transmitting sounds.

In developing a pedagogy that integrates the alphabetic and the auditory, Elbow encourages writers to read aloud to each other:

> When you read your writing out loud, you often see things in it that you don't see any other way. Hearing your own words out loud gives you the vicarious experience of being someone else. Reading your words out loud stresses what is most important: writing is really a voice spread out over time, not marks spread out in space. The audience can't experience them all at once as they can a picture; they can only hear one instant at a time as with music. (*Writing without Teachers* 82)

For Elbow, reading aloud to a group highlights the role of audible voice in writing. It attunes the writer to how her text sounds to others; it attunes the reader to how linearity and timing play a role in writing just as they do in speech.

In the reading-aloud exercise, Elbow ultimately aims to create a liminal space between writing and speaking, reading and hearing. In our current digital moment, I would argue that sound editing emerges as the new technologically mediated liminal space between the alphabetic and the auditory. To explore this, I will demonstrate how Elbow's reading aloud exercise can be enhanced and transformed through engaging digital audio technologies. With a free software program (Audacity) and a built-in computer microphone (or cell-phone microphone), a student can easily read aloud and record something that he or she has written. In the moment of reading aloud, this exercise is really not much different from Elbow's except the composer speaks to a microphone rather than to a live audience. By reading aloud to a microphone, the writer becomes conscious of how his or her writing "is really a voice spread out over time, not marks spread out in space" (Elbow, *Writing without Teachers* 82). Yet when the writer stops reading, her voice no longer vanishes into the air. Rather, the writer's voice remains as marks (sound waves) spread out in space on a visual timeline (in a sound editor).

As the writer plays back her voice, she cannot only hear the texture of her voice (pace, accent, volume, rhythm); she can actually *see* her voice. When her volume rises, the sound waves visually rise. When she pauses, the sound waves become flat; the visual length of the flat space represents the time of pause. Although Elbow metaphorically suggests that reading writing aloud "can allow you to see things in it that you don't see any other way" (*Writing without Teachers* 82), the digital sound-editing process literally enables the writer to *see* aspects of her voice, such as silence, that are traditionally invisible. Furthermore, since the writer's recorded and played-back voice is produced by a machine and not by her body, the writer can "gain the vicarious experience of being someone else" (Elbow, *Writing without Teachers* 82)—of hearing how her words might sound to an audience. With digital audio tools, the writer can even actively begin to edit her voice. She can generate or eliminate silences; she can change pitch and volume; she can delete words, add words, and move words around. And then she can play back her words to see how they changed. In the end, the writer could use the digital sound-editing experience as way to revise—to *resee*—the voice of her alphabetic text.

In contrast to Elbow's focus on the importance of transforming alphabetic texts into spoken words, Otis Winchester's lesser-known expressivist textbook, *The Sound of Your Voice* (1972), highlights the ways alphabetic texts may be invented by recording speech. Winchester opens *The Sound of Your Voice* by establishing that listening closely to spoken words is one of the first steps in developing voice in writing:

> Begin listening to the sound of your conversational voice. Write down what you hear. Don't be put off by any seeming inarticulateness you hear. It may not be the most eloquent or efficient verbal communication, but it has served you well enough. So begin here. And as you listen to your voice and to the voices of others . . . begin to consider ways in which you might retain the fluency and immediacy of talk, yet increase the expressiveness of your written idiom. (Winchester 3)

In this way, Winchester suggests that students' conversational skills can be a powerful resource for their development as writers—that composition classes must help students explicitly draw connections between the related arts of speaking and writing. Although Winchester concedes that we should not just write as we talk, he suggests that participating in and listening to oral conversations can be a powerful method for inventing alphabetic texts. To this end, the first exercises in Winchester's book ask students to transcribe conversations in which they are participants or spectators—to "write as best you can from memory, or take down on the spot, or transcribe from a tape recording" (25).

Although Winchester suggests that analog tape recorders can be a useful tool for capturing conversations, he still asks students to transcribe their audiotapes so that they can more carefully analyze and ultimately revise the spoken words that they recorded. By asking students to translate their audio recordings into alphabetic text, Winchester seeks to help them "to retain the fluency and immediacy of talk, yet increase the expressiveness of their written idiom" (3). In an analog world, Winchester's emphasis on alphabetic transcription of audio was quite practical because very few people would have had access to the ability to edit audiotape. In the contemporary moment, however, it is increasingly possible that students could record their talk and then digitally edit it to enhance expressiveness (using free software such as Audacity). Updating Winchester's conversational pedagogy for the digital age, contemporary teachers might ask students to digitally record a conversation in which you are a participant. Listen to it multiple times. Cut and rearrange elements to make the conversation more concise and to highlight a particular aspect of it. Turn in the edited audio file, with an accompanying written reflection in which you discuss what the editing process taught you about the unique qualities of your voice and of the voices of others. Faced with the goal of substantially cutting the length of a recorded conversation, the student must necessarily listen carefully—listen repeatedly—to the words that were spoken. As a result, digital sound editing can be a powerful way to encourage students to critically reflect about the rhetorical effects of their spoken voices. In relistening to and remixing their conversations, students might also come to recognize the ways that oral dialogue can be a powerful form of invention—the ways they can discover new ideas through the process of talking with their peers.

To illustrate the potential inventive power of editing conversation, I am going to pause here to tell the story of my own experiences recording and editing conversations in which I've participated. And, as I tell this sound-editing story, my words will drift closer to the cadence of speech. . . . When I repeatedly relisten to my own conversational voice, I often become hyperaware of my speech patterns. I notice when I'm using unnecessary filler words. I notice when I'm pausing to think. I notice when I start making a point one way and then circle around and make it another way. I notice when I come to a moment of discovery—when I'm saying something I just realized through the process of conversing. I notice when I'm reflecting—when I'm rephrasing what my interlocutor said to make sure I'm hearing him or her correctly. I become conscious of when I'm talking too much and when I'm choosing not to talk. I notice when I'm constructing ideas collaboratively—when my conversation turns into a real dialogue.

And, as I listen repeatedly to my conversation, I start to make choices about what to keep, what to cut, and how to arrange it all. I make choices about what aspects of the conversation are worth sharing with others—what snippets of the conversation could stand alone without all the local context surrounding them. I make choices about which aspects of the conversation probably shouldn't be shared since they wouldn't really make sense or wouldn't really be compelling to someone who wasn't there. I make choices about how much I can cut while still retaining the "immediacy and fluency" of my talk. And, as I get close to the final edited product, I begin thinking of my conversation not as a time-bound, place-bound interaction, but as a carefully composed text that may be circulated to people I don't know in places I've never been. Quite simply, I start thinking of my conversation *as a piece of writing* that contains *the sound of my voice*.

In the above story, I draw upon Winchester's work to demonstrate how recording and editing conversation can help composers become more conscious of the rhetorical effects of their own spoken voices; in particular, I demonstrate how sound editing can enable composers to strategically select and arrange their spontaneous spoken words in order to "enhance their expressiveness" (Winchester 3). Although I see great value in reclaiming Winchester's attempt to help students draw connections between spoken conversation and alphabetic writing, I am concerned that his pedagogy (like Elbow's) focuses a bit too intently on teaching students to develop their own unique "personal idiom" (ix)—to pay attention first and foremost to the sound of their individual voice.

Seeking to turn down the volume of the individual speaking self and turn up the volume on the social practice of listening, I suggest that we place Winchester's expressivist voice pedagogy in dialogue with Krista Ratcliffe's feminist theory of rhetorical listening.

Ratcliffe demonstrates that rhetoric and composition theorists have traditionally emphasized speaking as "masterly expression, writing, a means of masterly expression, and reading a means of mastering-the-masterly expression. All three quickly subsume listening" (24). Ratcliffe critiques this emphasis on masterly expression because it reinforces patriarchal, Eurocentric structures in which those of privileged gender and race remove themselves from the necessity of listening to others. Seeking to counter the tradition of speaking, reading, and writing as mastery, Ratcliffe offers the practice of rhetorical listening as a way of naming "a person's conscious choice to assume an open stance in relation to any person, text, or culture" (26). Ultimately, Ratcliffe suggests that this kind of listening with openness can be a type of "interpretive invention" (17)—a way of developing politically responsible modes of language and action that are attentive to the power dynamics of race and gender.

Although Ratcliffe does not address audio recording in her discussion of rhetorical listening, her elucidation of the transformative political power of listening can help extend Winchester's conversational pedagogy in a feminist direction. In asking students to record and edit conversation, we can encourage them not only to pay attention to the sound of their voice but also to pay attention the political practice of their listening: What do you notice listening to the recorded conversation now that you did not hear before? When in this conversation do you feel you are listening or being listened to? How can you tell? What would this conversation sound like if you edited your own voice out of it? How do you think the person you conversed with might edit this conversation differently? How do power differentials of gender, race, and other categories of difference influence the practice of listening in this conversation? Traditionally, listening has been a very ephemeral act. We might be able to go back and carefully reread a text, but we have not been able to relisten to a conversation. Yet, the process of digital audio recording and editing enables—and even encourages—close repeated listening. By asking students to record and edit conversations in composition classes, we may be able to help them listen more attentively and more openly to the spoken words of others.

When we relisten to the voices of Winchester and Elbow, it becomes apparent that compositionists have a long tradition of drawing connections among writing, speaking, listening, and reading. Although expressivist voice pedagogies are often dismissed as focusing largely on cultivating the "authentic" self, we must remember that expressivist pedagogies of voice were about *sound* as much as they were about self. At this moment when digital technologies are once again pushing compositionists to attend to sound in our classes, it makes sense that we reclaim and critically extend the expressivist understanding of voice as a concept that encompasses both the alphabetic and the auditory.

TRACK 2: RHETORIC

While expressivist voice pedagogies offer auditory approaches for teaching personal writing, they tend not to emphasize the rhetorical process of adapting persuasive discourse to diverse audiences. As we consider ways that auditory forms of communication may be integrated into the teaching of persuasive writing, then, it can be helpful to revisit the rhetorical pedagogy of Edward P. J. Corbett. Although numerous composition historians have outlined Corbett's crucial role in adapting classical rhetoric to the teaching of alphabetic writing (Berlin; Connors, Ede, and Lunsford), they tend to pass over Corbett's simultaneous attempt to develop a rhetorical pedagogy that integrated the teaching of auditory and alphabetic forms of communication.

In seeking to reclaim classical rhetoric as a model for composition pedagogy, Corbett was acutely conscious of the fact that he was reviving a tradition that was initially developed to guide the analysis and production of persuasive speaking. For example, in the 1972 article, "Rhetoric, the Enabling Discipline," Corbett reminds teachers that "rhetoric, after all, had its beginnings as the art of oral discourse. It would be a gain for everyone concerned if the split that developed back in 1915 between teachers of English and teachers of Speech was repaired" (35). In Corbett's view, the revival of classical rhetoric ultimately necessitates a radical reimagining of the disciplinary division between speech and composition instruction.

In explaining why speaking should be included in composition classes, Corbett emphatically reminds teachers that many classical rhetorical concepts (such as *kairos*) are intimately tied to the practice of spoken oratorical performance:

> Classical rhetoric had its beginning as a practical course designed to train the citizen in the most effective way of composing a discourse that would be delivered *via voice* before a live audience. The speaker had to be aware of his audience, had to know it, had to know its attitudes, its emotional disposition, its aspirations and prejudices. It was the audience mainly that determined what a speaker would choose to say and how and in what order he would say it. The discourse of the Athenian forum was conceived as a communication art more intensely perhaps than at any time since. ("A New Look" 18)

In this way, Corbett suggests that compositionists should be wary of defining their work in terms of teaching students to produce particular kinds of written products; rather, compositionists should define their field as teaching students the process of analyzing and adapting to audiences—a process common to both spoken and written discourse. Indeed, Corbett seeks to remind composition teachers that spoken embodied performance (hearkening back to the Athenian forum) can be one of the best ways to teach the transferable skill of audience analysis—one of the best ways to make audience visible to students.

Further drawing connections between oratory and composition pedagogy, Corbett also suggests that experience with spoken performance can enhance students' understanding of the rhetorical construction of ethos. Hearkening back to the classical tradition of *progymnasmata*, Corbett notes that ancient rhetoricians taught students to manipulate ethos by having them craft and deliver speeches in which they impersonated other people (living, dead, or fictional). Corbett sees these impersonation exercises as valuable because they "forced the pupils to assume a new personality, a different mind-set, and to adopt words and sentiments that would be appropriate to the person being impersonated" (*Selected Essays* 206). Extrapolating from the classical tradition of having students impersonate famous orators, Corbett recommends that experience in acting can be beneficial for helping students develop an understanding of the use of ethos in speaking and writing: "I have often preached that acting is one of the best preparations for a speaker or writer. An actor must literally become another character, and during the two-hour traffic on the stage, he must think like, talk like, act and react like that other character" ("Rhetoric, the Enabling" 9). By learning how to consciously craft an ethos on the stage, students may also gain a richer understanding of possibilities for manipulating ethos on the page. Challenging the notion that the teaching of writing and the teaching of performance are two entirely separate realms, Corbett reminds compositionists that both actors and writers must make conscious choices about how to perform an identity (construct an ethos) for a particular audience and a particular purpose.

Although Corbett suggests that experience in spoken performance (acting) could help students learn about ethos construction in writing, I have not found any evidence that he taught acting in his classes; for Corbett, writing and acting were ultimately related though distinct curricular pursuits. In our contemporary digital classrooms, however, the lines between writing and acting are increasingly blurring. For example, in composing a digital audio essay or video essay, students often write and then perform a script; the success of the final video or audio product hinges as much on the delivery of the words (the voice and gesture) as it does on the words themselves. When we consider assessing these newer digital audio and video forms of composition, we often worry about what it is we are judging: the writing or the acting? Are we being seduced by an essay that is not very well written because it is well-performed? Are we being overly critical of an essay that is well-written because it is not well-delivered? Of course, all of the above questions rest upon the assumption that writing and acting are wholly unrelated activities—that experience in "acting" is irrelevant to the work of the writing class. Yet, if we listen to Corbett, we can remind ourselves that experience in acting can help students gain an understanding of ethos that they can potentially transfer to more conventional print composition—that writing and acting are dynamically interrelated rhetorical pursuits.

In addition to looking to Corbett for discussions of the inter-relation of writing and acting, we also might turn to James Moffett's classic 1968 text, *Teaching the Universe of Discourse*. Although Moffett's work emphasized personal, expressive writing more than Corbett's did, he shared with Corbett an interest in articulating the ways that experience with drama could help students to develop rhetorical consciousness. In Moffett's view:

> The guts of drama is rhetoric, people acting on each other; speech is featured, but nonverbal influence is highly prized, to say the least. A play is a model of how the student, his parent, friends and enemies do things to each other verbally and in conjunction with voice, gesture, and movement. In a play, communications are "live," existential; the personalities behind the words are most real, the intentions and ploys the most evident. Everything is present. Drama is the perfect place to begin the study of rhetoric. Confronted with a written monologue—a novel, essay, or treatise—a student deals with a phantom by comparison. An essay has a speaker who in turn has motives and ways of acting on his audience. But this action-at-a-distance will be much harder to respond to if the student has not been long accustomed, through experience with drama, to link words to speakers and motives. (116)

Like Corbett, Moffett argues that students can best understand the rhetorical dynamics of persuasion through participating in forms of embodied performance in which audience is made visible and all the available modes of persuasion (voice, gesture, movement) are employed. Once students have gained an understanding of the workings of persuasion in the vividly embodied setting of dramatic performance, they may then be able to transfer this rhetorical knowledge to the often more abstract process of persuading audiences through print.

Admittedly, Moffett's work was particularly addressed to K–12 teachers, so I can imagine that readers may wonder if experience in dramatics would really be relevant for the teaching of academic writing in the university. Certainly, college composition teachers may need to employ drama in different ways than teachers of younger students; however, I would still argue that dramatic activities can provide a bridge to help first-year university students understand difficult rhetorical concepts. For example, in my own first-year writing classes, I have often struggled with helping students to engage multiple perspectives on issues and to reflect critically about the ways they manipulate language to form arguments. To address these challenges, I've designed an assignment that asks students to compose a play script in which they imagine a conversation among three different people who hold differing positions on an issue or question. The script must include parenthetical citations to credit the sources for any facts or arguments they borrowed, but I ask that it be written in a more informal dramatic style. And, most crucially, during peer response sessions, students literally *perform* each other's scripts (and they are encouraged to make the texts come alive with voice and movement). In these performative peer response sessions, students often find problems or flaws in their arguments that they may not have noticed through more conventional silent reading. In the future, I intend to push the performative aspect further by actually having students turn their scripts into video or audio dramas, but even the simple in-class activity of staged reading has proved fruitful.

When we look back to the work of Moffett and Corbett, we can be reminded that rhetoric is a profoundly dramatic art that students have been practicing (informally) throughout their entire lives. In many cases, students already arrive in the composition class with a great deal of past experience rhetorically adapting their spoken words and embodied gestures in order to craft a particular kind of identity or argument for a particular audience. Rather than suggesting that this kind of everyday spoken performance is unrelated to the process of learning to write, we might instead help students draw connections between the art of spoken performance and the art of academic writing. For example, students might develop a more robust understanding of rhetorical appeals (ethos, pathos, logos) if they had the opportunity to compose and perform dramatic skits that demonstrate how these appeals are used in everyday life. Or, students might gain a richer sense of audience for their prose if they had the opportunity to *perform their words out loud* to an audience of their peers.[2] By making space for spoken performance activities in the composition class, we might ultimately enhance students' understanding of rhetoric as a practical art that can be applied both within and beyond the university classroom.

TRACK 3: DIALOGUE

Although Moffett's and Corbett's discussions of rhetoric productively emphasize that the teaching of language is a social phenomenon, they still tend to efface the political and ideological implications of rhetorical pedagogy. Seeking to place more emphasis on the ways that rhetorical practices can both reinforce and/or subvert hierarchical social structures, I turn to Ira Shor's classic 1980 text, *Critical Teaching and Everyday Life*—a text that James Berlin has credited with providing the "most complete realization" of social-epistemic rhetoric for the classroom ("Rhetoric and Ideology" 488). In engaging Shor's work, I ultimately hope to consider ways that multimodal composition pedagogies might be designed to help students come to both critically analyze and attempt to transform material hierarchies of class, gender, race, disability, and sexuality.

In developing his theory of critical composition pedagogy in *Critical Teaching in Everyday Life*, Shor was strongly influenced by Paulo Freire's pedagogical theories. Thus, in order to gain a nuanced understanding of the multimodal implications of Shor's pedagogy, it makes sense to look first to the roots in Freire from which Shor's work arose. In his classic *Pedagogy of the Oppressed*, Freire famously argues against a banking model of education, which positions students as empty vessels to be filled with the teacher's knowledge, proffering instead a problem-posing theory of education in which teachers and students collaborate together to analyze and attempt to transform oppressive aspects of the students' reality. In contrast to the banking classroom where the "teacher talks and the students listen" (73), the dialogical classroom is a space where all students feel empowered to speak: "Dialogue is the encounter between men [*sic*], mediated by the world, in order to name the world. Hence, dialogue cannot occur between those who want to name the world and those who do not wish this naming—between those who deny other men the right to speak their word and those whose right to speak has been denied them" (88). Challenging the academic tradition of viewing print texts as the most authoritative sources of knowledge, Freire ultimately argues for a literacy pedagogy grounded in spoken dialogue in which students and teachers collaboratively come to name and transform the world (at least in part) through the process of speaking and listening to one another. Although Freire does seek to teach students how to read and write print texts, he is very careful not to set up a hierarchy that privileges print forms of knowledge over aural, dialogic forms of knowing—a hierarchy that would reinforce the notion that "illiterate" peasants are mere empty vessels to be filled with knowledge from their print-literate teachers. For Freire, spoken dialogue is not just a means to the end of alphabetic literacy (a tool that literate teachers can employ to help students develop reading and writing skills); rather, spoken dialogue is a key component of the critical process of reconstructing education as the practice of freedom.

Echoing Freire, Shor also strongly emphasizes the value of spoken dialogue as an end in and of itself. In surveying the lives of working-class students in the 1970s, Shor notes that students rarely have the ability to engage in dialogue in the antidemocratic, institutional environments of the workplace and school:

> In the important institutional settings of mass culture, there is little dialogue and many commands. Thus, the official side of life includes an enforced silence which dishabituates people from gaining the experience of group discussion of policy. . . . Because a power struggle surrounds the use of words in every institution of life, there are tense rules and high prices to pay for talking. At the very least, supervisors discourage people from talking to each other because it interferes with productivity; in school, teachers dissuade students from talking to each other, or out of turn, not only to maintain order but also to maintain the teacher as the sole regulator of the talking. (72)

In order to enable students to come to recognize and challenge oppressive social structures, Shor suggests that critical teachers need to help students develop abilities in (and comfort with) the process of engaging in spoken dialogue in institutional settings—that they need to teach students strategies to resist the "enforced silence" (72) of the workplace, the school, and indeed the broader polis. For Shor, it is not enough just to engage students in writing critically about the world; compositionists also need to engage students in talking critically (dialoging) about the world.

Rather than positioning the teaching of speaking (dialogue) and the teaching of writing as wholly separate activities, Shor seeks to teach students to draw connections "between their speaking language and the act of writing language on paper" (131). In particular, Shor suggests that teachers engage students in composing alphabetic text through a collaborative oral process of dictation: "The dictation sequence begins by asking students to break into groups of two. One member of the team will be dictating his or her verbal thoughts on the theme for composition, while the second member of the unit will record, on paper, verbatim, what the person speaks. Then, the two change places, the recorder becoming the speaker, and the speaker becoming the composer" (131). In addition to emphasizing how dictation can help students draw on the resources of speech to produce alphabetic text (131), Shor also argues that dictation activities can help lay the groundwork for spoken classroom dialogues. In particular, Shor notes that dictation is "a style of writing that encourages peer relations. The students have to cooperate to get the work done; the teacher does not monitor them. They need to listen carefully to each other, something they are conditioned against through the teacher-centered schooling of their pasts" (131). Challenging the conventional understanding of writing as a silent, individual activity, Shor powerfully argues that critical teachers should work to help students come to reimagine writing as a collaborative auditory process that depends as much on listening to peers as it does on listening to the self.

In addition to exploring collaborative dictation as a classroom activity, Shor (along with Freire) also experimented with recorded conversation as a way of composing scholarly books. In the mid-1980s,

Shor and Freire audio-recorded numerous conversations about liberatory pedagogy. Shor then (in consultation with Freire) transcribed the audiotapes and edited the transcripts in order to create a "talking book" (Shor and Freire, xi). In the opening of their talking book, *Pedagogy of Liberation*, Shor and Freire take turns discussing their reasons for choosing to compose a book through recording an oral dialogue. Shor points out that the idea for the book arose from questions he and Freire had often been asked in conversations with teachers about dialogic pedagogy—that their "talking book" is ultimately an attempt to continue an ongoing spoken dialogue (Shor and Freire 2).

Extending Shor's justification for the talking book, Freire asserts that composing through spoken dialogue is a powerful way to provoke complex thought. Challenging the common notion that a recorded conversation is a less rigorous scholarly form than a solo-authored monograph, Freire argues that

> In the last analysis you are re-creating yourself in [spoken] dialogue to a greater extent than when you are solitary writing, seated in your office, or in a small library. And from the human perspective, the need for dialogue is so great, that when the writer is alone in the library, facing the blank sheets in front of him or her, the writer needs at least to mentally reach the possible readers of the book even if there is no chance that he or she will ever meet them. . . . Here in our case, we are facing uncountable, unknown readers, facing them symbolically, but we are one in front of another, you [Shor] and I. In a sense, I am already your [Shor's] reader and in a sense you are already my reader. . . . The mutual possibility to read ourselves before writing can make our writings better, because in this interaction we can change ourselves in the very moment of the dialogue. . . . Dialogue seals the act of knowing, which is never individual, even though it has an individual dimension. (3–4)

For Freire, all knowledge (even the knowledge expressed in books) is profoundly social—the result of a dialogue between writer and reader, composer and audience. Yet, when writers work silently alone, it is easy for them to forget the dialogic aspects of the process, ignoring the ways in which their words are ultimately shaped by their social interactions with others. In contrast, the process of composing a book through recorded conversation foregrounds how our words are always uttered in response to (in dialogue with) others. In discussing how the talking book genre highlights the social dynamics of writing, Freire implicitly suggests that recording and editing conversation (creating talking books or talking essays) can be a powerful tool to engage students in exploring composing as a social, dialogic act.

Working in the mid-1980s, Shor and Freire had limited access to equipment for editing and distributing audio; thus, it made sense for them to transcribe their dialogues into alphabetic text and then publish them in printed form. In the contemporary digital environment, however, the technologies of digital audio editing are much more available. As I discussed in track 1, composers can potentially employ free software such as Audacity to digitally edit their recorded dialogues (adding, deleting, and rearranging words) without the need for transcription. Rather than publishing the dialogue as a print text, composers could instead publish the final dialogue to the web as a single digital audio file or series of audio chapters. By releasing their digital dialogue under a creative commons license ("Get Creative"), composers could even invite audience members to remix the dialogues, literally adding their own voices to the conversation.

If we want to teach students to listen carefully to one another and to value spoken dialogue as a form of making knowledge (as Shor and Freire ask us to do), it makes sense to engage students in the process of collaboratively composing digital "talking essays." Working in small groups, students could digitally record themselves having a conversation about a problem they all encounter in their everyday lives. After importing the digital recording into a computer-based audio editor, students could then work individually or collaboratively to edit the conversations. In the process of editing, students might:

- add in additional spoken words (what they didn't get a chance to say originally or ideas they had only after engaging in and relistening to the dialogue);

- highlight moments when they were learning from one another (moments when their ideas were transformed through dialogue);
- emphasize key areas of commonality and difference in the experiences of the group;
- create a concise summation of the dialogue that would be comprehensible and engaging for the rest of the class (the two-minute version of a twenty-minute conversation)

As students edited their spoken dialogues (deciding what to add, rearrange, and delete), they would of necessity have to listen repeatedly—and carefully—to their spoken interactions with their peers. If this repeated listening were to cause students to change their minds or develop new insights, they would have the opportunity to revise and extend their earlier spoken thoughts. In relistening to their spoken interactions, students could also come to reflect on the process of spoken dialogue itself. For example, students could try to pinpoint those speaking strategies that tend to invite participation in contrast to those speaking strategies that tend to silence others, considering ways they might endeavor to make future spoken dialogues more inclusive.

Of course, students are not the only ones who could benefit from recording and editing digital dialogues; this activity could also be very useful for teachers. We teachers might be able to learn much more from students if we had the opportunity to relisten to the comments they make in class. In addition, we might be able to learn more from our colleagues if we had the chance to relisten to their spoken words as well as to reread their writings.

Although composition teachers spend much time engaging in spoken dialogues with students and colleagues, we often tend to marginalize conversation as an ephemeral activity ancillary to our "real" work: the analysis and production of alphabetic texts. In evaluating students in composition classes, we usually base our grades almost entirely on assessment of written products (with perhaps only a small percentage given to oral participation). In evaluating our colleagues for hiring, tenure, and promotion, we tend to weight print publications much more heavily than spoken presentations or discussions.

When we look back at the work of Shor and Freire, however, we can begin to imagine ways to make a space for talking books and talking essays in our pedagogical and scholarly lives. Rather than conceptualizing spoken dialogue as solely a tool for inventing and revising alphabetic texts (student papers, scholarly essays), we might come to reimagine the digital spoken dialogue as a valuable scholarly product in and of itself.

TRACK 4: DIALECT

As we consider methods for integrating auditory forms of composing into writing classes, it is crucial that we work to respect, value, and build upon all of the diverse forms of language that students bring to our classrooms. To this end, I turn now to analyzing Geneva Smitherman's foundational 1970s scholarship about the politics of language in the teaching of English. In addition to remembering and highlighting the important ways that Smitherman critiqued the hegemony of "Standard English" in writing instruction, I also seek to revisit and reclaim her insistence that composition teachers must work to challenge the conventional privileging of print forms of knowledge in the academy.

In her foundational 1977 book *Talkin and Testifyin: The Language of Black America*, Smitherman argues persuasively and importantly that Black English (or African American Vernacular English) is a dialect that has its own grammatical rules, semantic structures, and modes of discourse—that Black English is a complex, semiotically rich form of communication.[3] Resisting the common belief that English teachers' notions of correctness are universal and natural, Smitherman powerfully demonstrates that the concept of "Standard English" is ultimately an ideological construct that works to reinforce material racial hierarchies. Rather than teaching students one supposedly "standard" model of correctness, then, Smitherman argues that English teachers should engage students in critical study of the social and political implications of the many diverse dialects spoken and written in the United States.

In the years following the publication of *Talkin and Testifyin*, numerous compositionists have built on Smitherman's work to design pedagogies that engage students in critically interrogating the political and ideological implications of language use in both speaking and writing—powerfully demonstrating the crucial importance of studying and valuing multiple dialects of communication in the composition classroom (Banks; Ball and Lardner; Campbell; Gilyard; Kinloch; Moss; Richardson; Smitherman and Villanueva; Wible). [4] In many ways, the scholarship about language diversity in our field has always already entailed a robust multimodal exploration of the intersections between speaking and writing; yet, with a few notable exceptions (Banks; C. Selfe "Movement"), Smitherman's foundational work on African American language has rarely been cited in contemporary calls for a *digital* multimodal turn in composition pedagogy. If we look closely at Smitherman's foundational 1970s scholarship, however, we can come to remember that she powerfully outlined a capacious rhetorical pedagogy for integrating the study of auditory and alphabetic forms of communication—a pedagogy that remains timely and relevant in the contemporary digital, multimodal moment.

Challenging the tendency of many English teachers to view print forms of knowledge as the most authoritative, Smitherman's work repeatedly highlights the importance of oral forms of knowledge making in American life. For example, in *Talkin and Testifyin*, Smitherman asserts that

> in Black America, the oral tradition has served as a fundamental vehicle for gittin ovuh. That tradition preserves the Afro-American heritage and reflects the collective spirit of the race. Through song, story, folk sayings, and rich verbal interplay among everyday people, lessons and precepts about life and survival are handed down from generation to generation. . . . If we are to understand the complexity and scope of black communication patterns, we must have a clear understanding of the oral tradition. (73–74)

In this sense, it is not enough just to add print literature by African Americans to the canon; if English teachers truly wish to engage deeply with African American cultural production, they must *also* make a space for auditory forms of communication. In addition to teaching students about the usefulness of print writing, English teachers must *also* ask students to critically consider the ways that "written documents are limited in what they can teach about life and survival in the world" (*Talkin* 76).

Although Smitherman emphasizes the key role of oral traditions in African American knowledge production, it is crucial to note that she also strongly points to the importance of valuing the distinctive linguistic traditions of African American writers. Rather than setting oral discourse and print writing in opposition to one another, Smitherman ultimately wishes to highlight and to celebrate the ways oral and alphabetic traditions *interanimate* one another in African American life. For example, in *Talkin and Testifyin*, Smitherman includes numerous excerpts of print works of African American literature that draw upon and transform oral traditions of storytelling and call-and-response; in this way, Smitherman powerfully demonstrates that African American oral traditions and print literatures should be studied in relation to one another—that English teachers should resist their new critical tendency to remove print texts from the diverse auditory contexts in which they are produced and received.

Highlighting the limitations of print media as a form of communication, Smitherman's work frequently calls attention to the incredible challenge of attempting to represent the richness of African American oral traditions using the medium of alphabetic text. For example, in a 1974 column for *English Journal*, Smitherman notes that "since Black Idiom is the 'dialect of my nurture,' and since I believe in the legitimacy of ALL dialects of American English, uhm gon run it down in the Black Thang. Course this ain gon be totally possible due to the limitations of print media, but uhm gon be steady tryin" ("Soul 'n Style" 63.216). In this way, Smitherman deliberately breaks the conventions of standardized English writing in order to follow both the grammar and the *phonology* of Black English. And yet she also recognizes that some of the nuances of the African American oral tradition will be lost when she attempts to transliterate Black English speech to print.

Offering a powerful example of one aspect of the African American oral tradition that cannot adequately be represented in print media, Smitherman details the importance of tonal semantics—the complex ways that speakers of African American dialect manipulate the sounds of language in order to convey meaning. In *Talkin and Testifyin*, Smitherman explains that tonal semantics:

> refers to the use of voice rhythm and vocal inflection to convey meaning in black communication. . . . The speech rhythms and tonal inflections of Black English are, of course, impossible to capture in print. But you have heard these rhythms in the speech-music of James Brown and Aretha Franklin, in the preaching-lecturing of Martin Luther King, Jr., and Jesse Jackson, in the political raps of Stokely Carmichael and Malcolm X, in the comedy routines of Flip Wilson and Richard Pryor. The key to understanding black tonal semantics is to recognize that the sound of what is being said is just as important as "sense." (*Talkin* 134–35)

By highlighting the powerful ways that tonal semantics is used to make meaning in African American dialectical speech, Smitherman ultimately suggests that English instructors need to pay more attention to the auditory dimensions of communication. If students are limited to reading and writing only print texts, they will find it difficult to learn about and draw upon such semiotic resources as tonal semantics in order to communicate.[5] From Smitherman's point of view, it is not enough to read Martin Luther King and Stokely Carmichael; we must also teach students to *listen* to the ways they draw on African American oral traditions in delivering their words. It is not enough to make space for students to use the rhetorical forms of Black English in their writing; we must also make room for students to *perform* Black English (and other spoken dialects).

In addition to discussing the importance of attending to tonal semantics, Smitherman's *Talkin and Testifyin* also emphasizes the crucial role of oral storytelling as a form of knowledge making in African American life. In outlining a variety of oral storytelling traditions such as testifying and toasting, Smitherman asserts that spoken narrative is a powerful "black rhetorical strategy to explain a point, to persuade holders of opposing views to one's own point of view, and in general to 'win friends and influence people'" (*Talkin* 148). Arguing that English teachers should value and build upon African American students' experiences with oral storytelling, Smitherman powerfully contrasts an eighth-grade African American student's written paper about the 1967 Detroit riots with a taped interview with the student about the same subject. While the student's written paper was relatively simplistic in both style and content, the student's oral narrative (recorded in the interview) offered many more details and also employed "several sophisticated words and linguistic structures that did not appear in the theme" ("English Teacher" 63). In this way, Smitherman suggests that many young African American students have strong rhetorical abilities in oral storytelling that are not being recognized and built upon in their English classrooms. Rather than teaching students to see their experiences with oral storytelling as unrelated to the work of alphabetic writing, Smitherman suggests instead that teachers should help students consider ways they might draw upon their auditory rhetorical skills in the act of composing alphabetic text.

While Smitherman especially highlights the ways that a greater emphasis on speaking might benefit African American students in English classes, she also argues emphatically that instruction in the social and rhetorical aspects of speech is crucial for *all* students:

> Since students (both Black and white) will do far more speaking than writing in life after school—this applies even to college graduates—[some of] the English classroom's conventional written tasks should give way to speech activities. Specific assignments might involve simulation routines, such as job interview situations, panel discussions, debates, improvisational drama, and so on. Needless to say, listening skills should be stressed as an important counterpart to speaking. ("Soul 'n Style," 63.5 17)

Resisting the tendency of English teachers to devalue the teaching of speaking, Smitherman powerfully reminds instructors that auditory communication will play a crucial role in students' lives beyond the classroom as workers and citizens. As a result, English teachers should dedicate more time to helping students reflectively practice the rhetorical arts of speaking and listening using a variety of dialects.

Seeking to offer a rhetorical vision of pedagogy for integrating speaking and writing instruction, Smitherman's *Talkin and Testifyin* suggests that English teachers should focus attention on teaching students to develop "communicative competence." As Smitherman defines it,

> communicative competence, quite simply, refers to the ability to communicate effectively. At this point, however, all simplicity ends. For to be able to speak or write with power is a very complex business, involving a universe of linguistic choices and alternatives. Such a speaker or writer must use language that is appropriate to the situation and the audience. He or she must be able to answer such questions as: who can say what to whom, under what conditions? who is my audience? what assumptions can I make about that audience? what are its interests, concerns, range of knowledge? in a given act of speaking or writing, what examples and details will fit best and where? I am here talking about aspects of communication such as content and message, choice of words, logical development, analysis and arrangement, originality of thought and expression and so forth. Such are the real components of language power, and they cannot be measured or mastered by narrow conceptions of "correct grammar." (*Talkin* 228–29)

In outlining this vision of "communicative competence" as the goal of English pedagogy, Smitherman follows Corbett in asserting that an intensive focus on audience and rhetorical situation can form the basis for integrating instruction in speaking and writing. Smitherman, of course, also powerfully extends and revises Corbett's classical rhetorical approach by placing more emphasis on the importance of challenging supposedly universal notions of grammatical correctness—the importance of recognizing that rhetorically effective writing and speaking can be composed in a great variety of dialects. Furthermore, while Corbett points largely to classical orators and contemporary white men as models of rhetorical excellence,

Smitherman draws her rhetorical exemplars from a wide range of African American speakers and writers.

Smitherman demonstrates that we can learn much about rhetoric (about "communicative competence") by studying the collective use of tonal semantics and call-and-response patterns in African American sermons, by studying the persuasive uses of storytelling in African American conversation, by studying the rhetorical practice of the dozens, by studying the poetry of Nikki Giovanni, the oratory of Malcolm X, the plays of Amiri Baraka to name but a few sources. Rather than seeking to offer a universal model for integrating speaking and writing instruction (as Corbett and Moffett did), Smitherman's work calls us instead to collaboratively work with students to study a wide array of aural and alphabetic rhetorical practices in diverse cultural contexts—to explore the ways rhetorical practices both construct and are constructed by cultural knowledge and material hierarchies.

In addition to engaging students in analyzing work written in diverse dialects, Smitherman reminds us that we also need to teach students to analyze a wide range of auditory rhetorical practices: political oratory, sermons, hip-hop songs, everyday conversations, personal stories, protest chants, and so on. For example, in addition to asking students to read the text of Malcolm X's famous "Ballot or the Bullet" speech, we should also ask them *to listen carefully* to an audio recording of the speech—paying attention to the ways tonal semantics and patterns of call-and-response contribute to its persuasive power. Furthermore, we might ask students to use digital audio technologies to investigate patterns of oral language use in their home communities. By recording speech events and conducting interviews (with permission), students could gather data about language use, analyze that data, and then edit it along with spoken commentary to create a kind of audio ethnography. Quite often, students find it difficult to reflect about the social implications of their speech because many of their aural rhetorical practices are largely unconscious. By asking students to record speech events and then relisten to them, we might enable them to make more robust and complex arguments about ways of speaking in their own communities.

Although Smitherman's work focuses attention particularly on making classrooms inclusive for African American students, she also emphatically notes that English teachers must come to value "ALL dialects" of English ("Soul 'n Style," 63.2 16). We should remember that oral traditions play an important role in the lives of students from many different cultural backgrounds. Furthermore, with the increasing globalization of English, the number of English dialects that students are likely to encounter is increasing, making it even more crucial that we integrate analysis of diverse forms of speech into the composition class. Ultimately, if we seek to prepare students to communicate effectively in a diverse, globalizing world, we must come to question both the hegemony of standardized English and the hegemony of print—must come to craft pedagogies that enable students to make and to listen to knowledge conveyed through diverse forms of dialectical speech.

TRACK 5: REPRISE

Although digital audio technologies offer new possibilities for integrating aurality and composition instruction, we must remember that the teaching of writing has always already been an auditory art. When we look back at many of the foundational texts of expressivist, rhetorical, and critical pedagogy in our field, we can be reminded that compositionists have long sought to develop pedagogies that integrate the teaching of alphabetic and auditory communication. Whether we are teaching to foster personal voice, rhetorical awareness, or critical consciousness, we are ultimately pursuing pedagogical goals that cannot adequately be met by an exclusive focus on alphabetic text alone.

Refrain 1: Speaking and Writing Are Deeply Interconnected Social Activities

As Freire reminds us, participating in spoken dialogue is one of the most powerful ways to come to recognize that all knowledge—both alphabetic and auditory—is ultimately socially constructed. If we wish to teach writing as a social process, then, it's imperative that we highlight the important role that spoken conversation can play in the invention and revision of alphabetic texts. Of course, I recognize that many composition teachers already incorporate a great deal of conversation into their teaching of writing: peer response groups, writing conferences, and oral discussion of readings and rhetorical concepts. I imagine (indeed, I hope) that most readers of this volume have long ago rejected the "banking model" in which teachers lecture to silent students. But, I would nevertheless assert that we could do more to help students come to recognize the power of spoken conversation as a tool for creating knowledge—as a tool for collaborative invention and revision.

In particular, I would suggest that we should strive to give students the opportunity to talk about their own writing during almost every course period so that they can recognize that spoken conversation is a key invention strategy to be employed during all moments of the composing process. For example, we can ask:

- student groups to read over a writing prompt, collaboratively generating a list of questions about aspects of the assignment that they find unclear or challenging.
- pairs or small groups of students to collaboratively brainstorm a list of possible ways of approaching a new assignment.
- pairs of students to audio-record their plans for drafting.
- peer response groups to audio-record their discussions of drafts, and then edit their recordings in order to select the three key ideas for revision that each writer received.
- each student in class to state aloud the key argument of their paper draft in one minute or less.
- pairs or small groups of students to read a paragraph of their peer's writing aloud and then to work collaboratively to revise it for voice and style
- individual students to keep a digital journal where they note all of the out-of-class conversations about their writing they have had with roommates, friends, parents, and others (perhaps using a mobile phone as a convenient technology for recording notes on the fly).

- individual students to translate their paper draft into a five-minute oral presentation (performed in front of a peer group).
- pairs of students to audio-record interviews of each other about their process of composing a paper (as invention for a reflective essay or writer's memo).

In the list above, I offer just a few options (some well established, some more novel) that teachers might use in order to help students come to value and to employ spoken conversation as a robust technique for inventing and revising alphabetic texts. Although I place a special emphasis on the possibilities of digital audio recording as a tool for turning up the volume on auditory techniques for invention and revision, I would argue that it can also be very valuable to have students take alphabetic notes about their conversations (as Ira Shor did). After all, we must remember that some students may not have access to audio recording technologies (newer cell phones, laptops) or may not feel comfortable recording their voices; as a result, the technology of alphabetic note taking may remain the best option for recording spoken conversations in many cases. Ultimately, what is most important is that teachers: 1) provide students with copious opportunities to talk about their writing; 2) encourage students to record (via alphabetic or audio means) key moments in their spoken conversations; 3) explicitly engage students in discussion of how they can employ spoken conversation as a transferable invention strategy for all of the future writing they will complete (in the university and beyond).

Refrain 2: Spoken Performance Is a Useful Tool for Developing Rhetorical Awareness

By engaging in spoken performance, students can learn much about ways to consciously construct an identity (an ethos) for a particular audience and purpose. Rather than seeing instruction in speaking as a distraction from the teaching of writing, we might instead follow Corbett, Moffett, and Smitherman in exploring how experience with public speaking and performance might help students develop transferable rhetorical skills that they could apply to the production of alphabetic texts. In particular, I would suggest that teachers should consider including at least one formal auditory performance assignment in the writing class as a way to heighten students' rhetorical awareness of audience. For example, teachers might assign students to give a live presentation that makes an argument similar to one they plan to make in a future alphabetic paper. In crafting and delivering their presentations, students should be encouraged to employ whatever dialects and speech genres they need in order to best convey their argument to their audience.

In addition to asking students to give live presentations in class, teachers might also ask students to craft a digital audio essay in which they consciously compose and deliver spoken words in order to persuade a particular audience beyond the classroom—making use (once again) of whatever speech genres and dialects are crucial for delivering their message. In crafting an audio essay, students will often first write a script of the words they intend to say, but they must carefully revise and practice their script in order to make it suitable for spoken delivery. Students should be encouraged to read their scripts aloud multiple times and to perform their rough scripts for their peers—taking care to revise their words so they will be persuasive, engaging, and clear to an audience who are listening to them only once.[6]

To help students gain a heightened sense of audience, teachers can ask students to present their audio essays in front of the whole class. During the workshop, the students play their audio essay for the class and then have a chance to watch their peers respond in real time—to see the places where they laugh, where they seem bored, where they seem confused, where they seem most engaged. After the class listens to an audio essay, they then engage in dialogue with the composer, considering questions such as:

What is the argument of this essay?
What parts of this essay confuse you?
What is most memorable about this essay?
How does the spoken delivery of the words contribute to or
    detract from the meaning?

What parts of this essay were most engaging to hear? And
least?

How could the speaker add more complexity or nuance to
their argument?

Ideally, the composer of the audio essay will have the chance to ask
questions and provide clarifications—the chance to collaboratively
reinvent his or her essay through process of engaging in dialogue
with the class. In many ways, the audio essay can be a powerful
method for introducing auditory rhetoric into the composition class
because it blurs the boundaries between speaking and writing. On
the one hand, students have the chance to experiment the unique
rhetorical affordances of spoken delivery—to consider ways vocal
tone, rhythm, and pitch may be employed to make meaning. On the
other hand, students also have the chance to carefully compose and
rework their words over time (by writing, revising, and reperforming
their alphabetic script). In this sense, the audio essay constitutes a
kind of hybrid aural/alphabetic genre that is particularly appropriate
for the composition class because it can help students develop both
speaking and writing skills at the same time.

Refrain 3: An Inclusive Pedagogy Necessitates
Questioning the Hegemony of Print
When we require students to read and write only print texts, we
greatly limit the kinds of experiences they can draw upon to make
knowledge in their school-based writing. If we wish to create classrooms that welcome all the diverse bodies of knowledge that students
bring to the classroom, we must enable students to employ auditory
modalities of research (such as interviews and oral storytelling). The
inclusion of auditory forms of knowledge making in composition
may be particularly helpful for students who come from cultural
backgrounds that place a high value on oral tradition as a way of
making and recording knowledge.

When we introduce students to conducting research, then, we
should encourage them to consider employing oral interviews as a
way of capturing forms of community knowledge that are often
not written down. For example, if a student wanted to study the

ways that texting was influencing the communication practices of young adults, she might gain more valuable information by talking with her friends than she would if she limited herself only to reading the latest Pew study. If a student wanted to understand how gentrification was transforming her neighborhood, she might gain different insights from interviewing her grandparents than she would by engaging solely alphabetic sources on the topic. By having students engage in oral interviewing as a kind of research, we can help them recognize that spoken conversation is a powerful way of recording and sharing knowledge about communities—that we unnecessarily limit our perspective on the world if we value only knowledge that has been codified in alphabetic text. Ideally, students would audio-record their interviews so they could capture the exact words of their informants. Students could then transcribe quotations from their interviews to include in alphabetic papers, *or* they could edit the interviews (along with voiceover commentary) in order to create a digital audio documentary. In addition to asking students to conduct and edit interviews of community members outside of class, we also might engage students in recording and editing dialogues among themselves—creating the kinds of "talking essays" I described in track 3.

When we offer students the opportunity to compose audio texts in composition, we productively destabilize the conventional academic notion that alphabetic writing is the most authoritative, the most important form of knowledge making. Ultimately, if we wish to create an academy that values the diverse literacies and knowledges of *all* students, we need to make room in our courses for students to compose with multiple modalities—room for students to construct and share knowledge that cannot adequately be conveyed through print alone.

Part Two

"All Media Were Once New," or The Technologies Composition Forgot

3

The First Time Print Died: Revisiting
Composition's Multimedia Turn (1967–74)

IN A 2004 ARTICLE IN *CCC*, Kathleen Blake Yancey asserts that compositionists are living in a unique moment in which literacy "is in the midst of tectonic change" (298). Placing a particular emphasis on the ways that shifts in communication technologies are transforming definitions of writing, Yancey argues that "never before has the proliferation of writings outside the academy so counterpointed the compositions inside. Never before have the technologies of writing contributed so quickly to the creation of new genres" (298). Of course, Yancey is far from being the only contemporary scholar to argue that we are living in a moment when shifts in communication technologies are causing a disconnect between the composition classroom and the literacy practices of students. Within the past ten years, we have seen many calls for compositionists to engage students in using digital technologies to compose multimodal texts that blend images, words, and sounds in associative ways (D. Anderson; George; Kress; Takayoshi and Selfe; WIDE; Wysocki). Clearly, many in the field are in agreement with Yancey that we in composition "have a moment" (297).

In this chapter, I seek to turn our field's attention to a previous moment—1967 to 1974—when many teachers of writing were concerned, like Yancey, that shifts in communication technologies necessitated a rethinking of composition's exclusive focus on linear, alphabetic text. Just as Yancey suggests that emerging digital technologies have resulted in a proliferation of multimodal genres of writing, compositionists in the late 1960s and early 1970s were concerned that the electronic revolution had produced a generation

of students who were more interested in multimedia forms of composing—the film, the television program, the comic—than in
writing conventional print texts. Indeed, in journal articles and
composition textbooks published from 1967 to 1974, we can uncover
numerous compositionists engaging similar concerns and making
similar arguments to the ones many scholars are making today.

At the turn of the 1970s, numerous compositionists argued that
writing courses would cease to be relevant unless they paid attention to visual and multimedia texts (Briand; Clare and Ericksen;
Corbett; Frank; Hutchinson; P. Mahony; Murphy; Sego). Although
most compositionists of the late 1960s and early 1970s focused on
visual and multimedia texts as objects of analysis, some scholars
in this time period also proposed that writing teachers engage students in *producing* visual and multimedia texts (Clare and Ericksen;
Burnett and Thomason; Kytle; Murphy; Sparke and McKowen;
Wiener). Furthermore, a few compositionists of the early 1970s
suggested that the electronic revolution necessitated a rethinking
of the field's conventional privileging of linearity and originality
in print texts, arguing instead that writing teachers should engage
students in analyzing and/or producing participatory, associative
texts that made meaning through juxtaposition, incorporated found
images and words, and enabled audience interaction (Kytle; Lutz;
Sparke and McKowen).

Although I agree with Yancey that our current digital moment
is unique, I nevertheless would contend that contemporary compositionists have much to learn from our field's previous electronic
moment—much to learn from the mostly forgotten ways that writing teachers sought to transform their pedagogical practices and
materials to account for the seemingly "new media" of film, television, and Xerox machines. In these past pedagogical experiments, we
can find some "lost threads" (Dunn) that can help us reimagine our
digital work; we may not be able to adopt past pedagogical practices
unaltered, but we can use past practices as inventive heuristics for
rethinking our contemporary digital pedagogies. And, at the same
time, we can (with the advantage of hindsight) see some of the limi-

tations in arguments that past compositionists made about the new media of their day, causing us to question the limitations of some our own quite similar claims about the new media of our current moment. Finally, by recovering writing teachers' past experiments engaging new media before the rise of the personal computer, we can better elucidate the unique disciplinary expertise that we *as compositionists* bring to crafting new media texts that blend words, images, and sounds in associative ways.

Although the term "new media" is popularly used in reference to contemporary technologies such as digital video, blogs, and social networking sites, many scholars have argued that the study of new media should not be confined to the contemporary digital moment alone—that we can better understand new(er) digital media if we contextualize them in relation to old(er) media (Banks; Baron; Bolter and Grusin; Gitelman; McCorkle; Reid). As Lisa Gitelman and Geoffrey Pingree assert, we must be mindful that "all media were once new" (xi), and thus scholars will better be able to understand the contemporary dynamics of "new media" if we look back to past moments when other forms of media were first introduced. At moments when media are new, they tend to "pass through a phase of identity crisis, a crisis precipitated at least by the uncertain status of the given medium in relation to established, known media and their functions" (Gitelman and Pingree xii). As we once again face a moment of "crisis" as we encounter a generation of so-called "digital natives" (Prensky; Palfrey and Gasser) in the classroom, it can be instructive to investigate ways past composition teachers responded to the "crisis" of teaching a generation of students who had grown up watching television.

Seeking to historicize our field's current attempts to respond to technological change, I present here four multimedia tracks from turn-of-the-1970s composition—four tracks in which composition-ists grapple creatively with the waning significance of print literacy in the lives of their students. In track 1, "Classical Rhetoric for the Electronic Student," I listen carefully to the ways Edward P. J. Corbett engaged with Marshall McLuhan's theories of new media.

In particular, I suggest that Corbett's revival of classical rhetoric pedagogy reflected his *ambivalent* response to emerging technologies such as television. On the one hand, Corbett sought to demonstrate that classical rhetorical theories were particularly relevant to the multimedia forms of communication valued by youth. Yet, on the other hand, Corbett's revival of linear forms of oratory also represented an attempt to resist what he saw as they unnecessarily fragmented and illogical nature of much new media discourse.

In track 2, "Current-Traditional Multimedia," I explore how Esther Burnett, Sandra Thomason, and Harvey Wiener worked to integrate collages, photo essays, and cassette slideshows into composition courses—highlighting ways that multimedia composing could be used to enhance the invention of alphabetic texts. Although I consider how contemporary teachers might productively build upon this past multimedia work, I also turn a critical lens on how Burnett, Thomason, and Wiener at times employed new media in order to reinforce traditional (and sometimes problematic) pedagogical practices.

In track 3, "Inventive Juxtapositions," I analyze the multimedia turn in composition textbook design, focusing especially on the innovative integration of visual and alphabetic materials in William Sparke and Clark McKowen's *Montage: Investigations in Language* (1970). Whereas many multimedia textbooks in this period used visuals in supplemental ways, *Montage* usefully engaged students in both analyzing and *producing* visual texts, highlighting especially the inventive possibilities of juxtaposing words and images.

In track 4, "Composition as Assemblage," I engage Ray Kytle's largely forgotten 1972 *Comp Box* (a boxed collection of photocopied materials that students were invited to remix and extend). In particular, I argue that Kytle usefully crafted a multimedia pedagogy that engaged students in critically interrogating and challenging the ways that media texts construct reality—a pedagogy that might usefully inform contemporary attempts to integrate digital media production and cultural studies critique. In addition, I explore ways that Kytle's *Comp Box* productively destabilized conventional notions of "originality" and "linearity" in print texts.

TRACK 1: CLASSICAL RHETORIC FOR
THE ELECTRONIC STUDENT

In addition to advocating for the integration of speaking and writing in composition classes, Edward P. J. Corbett also argued that rhetorically minded compositionists should pay attention to "how electronic media have radically altered the ways in which we acquire, structure and express our knowledge of the world around us" ("Rhetoric in Search" 174). In seeking to understand how the teaching of rhetoric might need to change in light of emerging electronic media, Corbett frequently drew on the work of Marshall McLuhan ("Rhetoric of the Open" 289, 292; "Rhetoric in Search," 174–175; "What Is Being Revived," 172). Although Corbett at times expressed skepticism about some of McLuhan's more radical claims, he nevertheless also asserted "that Marshall McLuhan's book *Understanding Media* be made required reading for all teachers of English" ("What Is Being Revived," 172)—suggesting in particular that McLuhan could help teachers understand how the ubiquity of television was transforming the rhetorical practices of youth.

In many ways, Corbett's famous 1969 essay, "The Rhetoric of the Open Hand and the Rhetoric of the Closed Fist," represents his attempt to come to terms with his ambivalence about how shifts in communication technologies were influencing rhetorical practices. In this essay, Corbett compares the rhetoric of the Renaissance (the Gutenberg era) with the rhetoric of the 1960s (the electronic era). In contrast to the Renaissance focus on the linear printed text as the central form of persuasion, Corbett notes that 1960s youth privileged nonverbal, fragmentary means of persuasion in their attempts to argue persuasively for social change. Enumerating the many ways that young protestors employed music, visual posters, costumes, and other nonverbal modes of persuasion, Corbett notes somewhat regretfully that "words, of course, do play some part in these demonstrations, but words clearly play a subsidiary role, and it is notable how fragmentary these verbal utterances are" (292). Although Corbett is personally ambivalent about what he sees as the declining centrality of linear, alphabetic text in political discourse, he also tends to follow McLuhan in viewing the shift to nonverbal modes of communication as an effect of the proliferation of electronic media. In particular, Corbett asserts that the young demonstrators' turn away from the printed word "serves to confirm Marshall McLuhan's claim that the electronic media have expanded and intensified the human sensoria. Aural, visual, and tactual images have an immediacy, an intensity, a simultaneity about them that words strung out one after the other on a page can hardly achieve" (292).

As a rhetorician, Corbett knows that he has to adapt his message about classical rhetoric to the concerns of 1960s students, taking into account their "emotional disposition, aspirations and prejudices" ("A New Look" 18). Thus, Corbett sets out to demonstrate to students that classical rhetoric is in fact uniquely relevant to the electronic generation—that there are striking similarities between the world of Aristotle and the world of 1960s youth. Drawing on McLuhan, Corbett asserts that the electronic media are increasingly returning U.S. society to the "the audio-visual world in which rhetoric had its beginning. Technology, of course, has made it a different audio-visual world from what the Greeks knew, but it is still fundamentally the time-world of sound and icon that the Greeks knew rather than the space-world of graphic symbols that we have become accustomed to ever since Gutenberg invented the printing press" ("Rhetoric in Search" 174–75). In other words, classical rhetoric presents a viable model for the electronic age precisely because it was not initially designed for print—because it was developed in an age when auditory forms of communication were supreme.

In considering how classical rhetorical theories might inform the analysis and production of electronic media, Corbett focuses especially on elucidating the transferability of classical conceptions of audience analysis:

> If as McLuhan claims, electronic media are replacing typographical media as the principal means of informing, persuading, and entertaining the citizenry, we shall certainly have to develop a new rhetoric to serve this age. But I propose that a rhetoric of "hot" and "cool" electronic media has some valuable lessons to learn from Aristotelian rhetoric. And the most valuable lesson it can learn is Aristotle's insistence that the

audience is the chief informing principle in any kind of communicative discourse. ("A New Look" 19)

In Corbett's view, theorists of new media such as McLuhan focus so much on how communication technologies shape society (on how the medium is the message) that they neglect to consider the important role of audience in shaping electronic discourse. A student reading McLuhan might gain a heightened sense of how communication technologies are reshaping her social world, but she would not be likely to gain a strong understanding of how she might shape communication technologies to persuade particular audiences for particular purposes. In this way, Corbett implicitly asserts that the classical rhetorical techniques for analyzing an audience of a speech are not necessarily substantially different than the techniques required for analyzing the audience of a print or electronic composition. If students could become sensitive to the need to adapt to audience in one form of media, they might transfer that understanding of audience adaptation to their composing of other forms of media.

Although Corbett frequently called for compositionists to apply classical rhetorical principles to the analysis and production of electronic texts, it is important to note that his foundational textbook, *Classical Rhetoric for the Modern Student*, remained quite conventional. Indeed, the first two editions of the textbook (1965 and 1972) contained no images at all and largely avoided mention of electronic forms of discourse. While lack of time and space is certainly one reason Corbett didn't substantively engage new media in his textbook, it is also the case that Corbett was deeply ambivalent about the transformation in communication he was witnessing, at times even nostalgically wishing for a return to the Gutenberg era ("Rhetoric of the Open" 295). In many ways, Corbett seemed to want to use new media analysis as a creative hook for convincing students of the value of studying the classical rhetorical tradition, but he wasn't quite ready to use new media as an inventive method for rethinking the fundamental assumptions of the composition textbook or the writing assignment.

Although Corbett's conception of the influence of new media on writing instruction was somewhat limiting, I still would contend that it is important that we as field engage more deeply with the role that new media played in the classical rhetoric revival. When we look back at Corbett's writing from 1967 to 1972, we can come to recognize that compositionists have a long history of seeking to adapt the teaching of writing to shifts in communication technologies—a long history of exploring how we might draw on rhetorical theories to teach students to analyze and produce multimodal texts that blend images, words, and sounds. In other words, Corbett's work can remind us that considerations of new media should not be left to "computers-and-writing" or "technical communication" specialists alone; rather, we can come to see engaging new media as a central part of the disciplinary heritage and ongoing work of all scholars and teachers of rhetoric and composition.

TRACK 2: CURRENT-TRADITIONAL MULTIMEDIA

Whereas Corbett frequently called for compositionists to engage with new media in their classrooms, he provided very few practical pedagogical examples for how this might be accomplished. In contrast, numerous other compositionists in this period (Burnett and Thomason; Murphy; Wiener) published articles offering detailed descriptions of how they incorporated multimedia assignments (slideshows, photo essays, collages) into their composition pedagogies. In outlining and justifying their strategies for introducing multimedia production in composition, these scholars often positioned their work as an attempt to adapt composition instruction to respond to the visual preferences of a new generation of students who had grown up watching television; yet, at the same time, these multimedia advocates also worked hard to demonstrate that their technological innovations could ultimately serve the traditional goals of the writing class.

In a 1974 article in *College English,* Harvey S. Wiener offers a compelling discussion of ways to integrate multimedia composing (photo essays, collages, tape recording) into a traditional "modes of discourse" curriculum.[1] In particular, Wiener details how composition teachers can employ informal multimedia composing to help students invent ideas for modes-based writing assignments in personal narrative, description, and comparison/contrast. For example, in his classes, Wiener asks students to create a visual photo collage (using found images from magazines) in response to the question, "What Am I?"; he then asks the students to translate their imagistic collages into a personal essay on the same topic (569). In another exercise, Wiener suggests that students might take photos of a place as a way to gather specific details to include in a "descriptive" essay (573). In addition to discussing numerous ways that visual photography and collage might help students develop ideas for papers, Wiener also encourages the use of audio tape recording as a research technique. In particular, Wiener suggests that students might tape-record and transcribe interviews with high school students and college students—using quotes from these interviews as the basis for an alphabetic essay that "compares and contrasts" the experiences of the two groups (573).

In making the case for the value of integrating multimedia composing into the modes-based writing class, Wiener focuses especially on detailing the changing interests and backgrounds of young students. Positioning the 1970s as a moment of a crisis in print literacy, Wiener begins his article by boldly asserting:

> It is no news to anyone teaching college English today that students sitting before us make up a non-literary generation. . . . To the youngster plugged in to his transistor radio, transfixed before the technicolor ghosts of the tv screen, bombarded by magazine pictures of wild and erotic action—in all but a very transitory sense, for him the word is buried in a landslide of visual and aural excitement. (566)

In addition to noting that many students had grown up in a technological environment where visual and audio media increasingly seemed to be supplanting the written word, Wiener also suggests that many students have come to fear the act of alphabetic writing as a result of past school experiences when they were penalized (with the red pen) for making errors. Recognizing that students fears about "correctness" might make it difficult for them to employ the written word as a tool for developing ideas, Wiener argues that media compositions such as the visual collage "can involve the student in an unthreatening medium which gives him the chance to express his thinking without fear of penalty . . . it helps reduce self-consciousness and allows the growth of an element of creative expression that is often lost in the student's panic for correctness" (567). In this way, Wiener productively suggests that media compositions (collages, photo essays, tape-recorded interviews) can be a kind of bridge to print literacy for students who have had negative experiences composing with alphabetic text in the past.

In explaining why multimedia composing is a particularly powerful way to enhance students' creative expression, Wiener intriguingly emphasizes the potentially positive effects of the reality that most English teachers do not have any experience "correcting" or "grading" multimedia texts:

> as English instructors looking upon a student's collage or photo essay, which of us will say, "This is right" or "This is wrong"? Our responses are essentially emotional: although we would surely correct a dangling modifier or a misspelled word (as would every one of the student's previous English teachers) there is not much in a visual presentation that we would know how to grade or correct. Committed so to words, we are much less rigid in our responses to non-verbal impressions offered by students. (567)

Although Wiener celebrates multimedia composing for the ways it can encourage a focus on idea generation over error correction, he ironically never seems to consider that English teachers might also employ informal, low-stakes writing as way to help students overcome their panic for correctness. In Wiener's worldview (not uncommon at the time), it appears almost unthinkable that an English teacher could look past the errors in an alphabetic text to focus mostly on responding to the ideas; the only way Wiener can imagine to move beyond error-centered pedagogy is to incorporate visual and auditory invention activities that (temporarily) remove print from consideration.

While Wiener's advocacy of multimedia production in composition was certainly quite radical and innovative, his broader writing pedagogy was paradoxically quite conservative and traditional. After all, he made sure to demonstrate that multimedia composing could be used to help students learn to write relatively formulaic, modes-based essays; he assured teachers that the ultimate goal was still to teach students to produce error-free prose (and that of course English teachers must always "correct" every error in any piece of alphabetic writing that students complete). By demonstrating ways that his multimedia exercises could easily be integrated into current-traditional, modes-based curricula, Wiener strategically enhanced the likelihood that conventional teachers might be willing to adopt aspects of his approach.

Similarly seeking to show how new media composing could fit with traditional pedagogical goals, Esther Burnett and Sandra Thomason published an article in *CCC* in 1974 describing how they asked students to create multimedia presentations as a way to teach traditional research writing skills. As part of a course in which students both analyzed and produced examples of life writing, Burnett and Thomason gave students the opportunity to compose a cassette slideshow biography that included "a written story of about 1,350 words, a 10–15 minute audio track, and 50–70 slides" (427). For slides, students would take pictures of images from books, periodicals, and postcards, create their own sketches and title slides, and sometimes compose original photographs (427–28). For audio, students might include voiceover, background music, or historical audio clips (428). Students with access to audio mixing equipment might layer sounds on tape, while others might play a tape of music while reading their "voiceover" script live (429).

In explaining their choice to teach students to compose cassette slideshows, Burnett and Thomason emphasize that incorporating multimedia production could be a way to engage students who otherwise tend to find alphabetic writing boring—a way to make composition "relevant to their [the students'] world of movies and TV" (426). Revealing the ways that the multimedia slideshow can be motivating for students, Burnett and Thomason tell the story of one of their students, Jim Baker, who had "found English composition uncongenial" (426) until the slideshow project. Not only did Jim report that he really enjoyed producing a slideshow that was well received by peers and instructor; he also noted that "never have I worked so hard for any project" (429). This argument that students are often more motivated by multimedia projects is one that frequently recurs in twenty-first-century case studies of students' multimodal composing (D. Anderson; Ellertson; Ross). Although contemporary multimodal teachers tend to suggest that today's "digital natives" are unique in their preference for new media forms of composing, the 1970s work of Burnett and Thomason can remind us that students have long welcomed multimedia alternatives to conventional writing assignments.

In addition to highlighting the ways that cassette slideshow projects can enhance student motivation and engagement, Burnett and Thomason also seek to demonstrate that their project still teaches "the research and writing methods required for the term paper: the thesis sentence, outline, footnote references, and bibliography" (426). Although Burnett and Thomason strongly emphasize that the cassette slideshow can be used to teach conventional forms of alphabetic citation, they also suggest that their multimedia project can help the student develop additional technical "skills, with the camera, tape-recorder, and projector, even the copystand and mixer, so that he can produce a multimedia show on his own for other college classes and later, perhaps, for teaching, public relations, salesmanship or community service"(426). In this way, Burnett and Thomason position the cassette slideshow assignment as a way both to help students develop conventional research writing skills *and* to enable students to gain experience with the multimedia technologies of composing that were becoming increasingly common in school, civic, and workplace contexts.

In discussing the process of teaching the multimedia slideshow, Burnett and Thomason emphasize that the English teacher's role is primarily to help students with the development of the scripted narration for the presentation. (For assistance with the audio-visual technology, students were assigned to go to the "learning center" in the library). Demonstrating ways that English teachers' conventional expertise is still relevant to the project, Burnett and Thomason suggest that composition instructors can help students learn to write a script "for a listening rather than a reading public" as well as to consider how their images should be arranged to complement their spoken words (428). Finally, Burnett and Thomason insist that the student should be instructed "to clear his script with his English instructor for grammar, clarity, and pronunciation of difficult words" (429). In this way, Burnett and Thomason (not unlike Wiener) seek to demonstrate that their unconventional slideshow project can still ultimately serve the "current-traditional" goal of teaching students to compose error-free products. Although the English teacher may not be an expert in the technology of slideshow composition, Burnett and Thomason assert that the writing instructor should still remain the ultimate arbiter of correct grammar, spelling, and pronunciation. In this sense, Burnett and Thomason's "innovative" slideshow pedagogy can be seen as somewhat conservative—especially when we consider that their article was published in *CCC* in the same year as the "Students' Right to Their Own Language" statement (coauthored by Smitherman).[2]

In recovering the history of the cassette slideshow, I seek on the one hand to demonstrate that compositionists have a rich heritage of teaching students to craft scripted narration for multimedia narratives—a heritage that substantially predates the contemporary digital turn in the field. Yet, I also think that the history of the cassette slideshow can remind us to be wary of the ways that multimedia projects can be problematically designed to "force the new media to do the work of the old" (McLuhan and Fiore 81). After all, Burnett and Thomason conceived of the cassette slideshow primarily as a way to teach the conventional term paper by other means. Rather than viewing the multimedia turn as an opportunity to rethink the assumptions of their seemingly error-driven, product-centered pedagogy, Burnett and Thomason instead sought primarily to use new media as a way to make writing term papers more interesting for students. Similarly, Harvey Wiener worked hard to fit his media composition assignments into a traditional "modes of discourse" approach, neglecting to consider ways that new media might cause us to question the rigid categories of modal pedagogy. Although it certainly can be useful to employ new media as way to make existing composition pedagogies more engaging, it also can be important to remain open to the ways that new media might enable us to reinvent what it means to teach composition—as the teachers I discuss in tracks 3 and 4 did.

TRACK 3: INVENTIVE JUXTAPOSITIONS

At the same time as scholars such as Wiener, Burnett, and Thomason were publishing academic articles about electronic rhetoric and pedagogy, many compositionists were composing "multi-media textbooks" (Sego) for use in writing classes. Especially in the period from 1970 to 1972, there were numerous composition textbooks published that incorporated a wide range of media texts, such as photographs, film scripts, comics, cartoons, advertisements, music scores, and paintings (Clare and Ericksen; Dunstan and Garlan; Frank; Hutchinson; Kytle; Mahoney and Schmittroth; Sparke and McKowen).

Although these multimedia textbooks were unusual for the diversity of visual and alphabetic selections they included, most of them remained quite conventional in arrangement, consisting of a series of separate units with accompanying pedagogical apparatus (commentary on selections, assignment prompts, questions to consider). In contrast, William Sparke and Clark McKowen's 1970 *Montage: Investigations in Language* greatly pushed the boundaries of conventional textbook design, seeking to create an interactive, nonlinear experience that could enable students to invent ideas through creative juxtaposition. In contrast to conventional methods for organizing textbooks, *Montage* includes no table of contents, no chapters or unit divisions, and no conventional headnotes explaining the selections. The central premise of the book is spelled out on the second page: "There is only one way in which a person acquires a new idea: the combination or association of two or more ideas he already has into a new juxtaposition in such a manner as to discover a relationship among them of which he was previously unaware. AN IDEA IS A FEAT OF ASSOCIATION" (Sparke and McKowen 2). These sentences are so clearly central to the book that they are repeated a few words at a time from pages 3 to 41 (often in large colored font superimposed over other alphabetic and imagistic selections).[3]

Whereas most multimedia textbooks in this period tended to separate imagistic and alphabetic selections (or to use images to illustrate alphabetic concepts), *Montage* often juxtaposed images and words in more complex, nuanced ways. For example, throughout the first thirty-nine pages of the book, the authors occasionally include roughly cutout images of common objects—plate fragments, locks, soap bubbles, wood—that seem to have no obvious relation to the text on the pages where they appear. On page 44, however, all of these objects are reassembled to make a human head that appears along with the caption, "combination." In this way, the "montage head" demonstrates the importance of reading the text in a nonlinear manner, looking not just at how everything on one page or in one chapter is connected but rather looking at how fragments from diverse pages might be reassembled to create new compositions. Of course, in the case of the "montage head," the authors of the book have already done the reassembling for the student. Later on in the book, however, the authors offer a blank "do it yourself head" that they encourage students to fill with images that represent their experience of engaging the textbook (292). In many ways, the recurring image of the "montage head" (or brain) presents an implicit argument about the associational nature of cognition—an argument that the process of invention involves making connections among disparate words and images in our minds.

In addition to emphasizing the ways that visual images (photographs, drawings, paintings, film stills) may be juxtaposed to create new ideas and compositions, *Montage* also seeks to heighten students' awareness of the rhetorical aspects of typography. Throughout the book, the authors juxtapose a relatively standard, black sanserif font (for body text), with diversely colored, large, script and serif fonts (often layering words in one font directly over words in another font). Breaking standard conventions for typographic alignment, *Montage* often features blocks of text that are slanted or even upside-down. Whereas typographical choices might pass unnoticed in more conventional texts, *Montage* almost demands that its readers consider the rhetorical effects of typography.

Revealing their strong interest in teaching students to analyze the visual aspects of printed texts, Sparke and McKowen encourage teachers to engage students in producing their own magazines. In addition to suggesting that students could write and edit magazine articles, Sparke and McKowen note that

> students can also gain insights into the visual aspects of a magazine by creating layouts. Teams of students can be assigned to suggest photographs and artwork (including cartoons) and to decide on the content, size, and placement of the illustrations. Type should also be considered. A printer can be invited to the class to discuss and demonstrate the various type families. (*Teacher's Manual* 46)

In this way, Sparke and McKowen quite radically assert that the teaching of writing necessarily entails the teaching of visual design—that students should have the opportunity to consider how choices of typography and/as image might alter or enhance the writing that they compose. Although many scholars have pointed to the rise of digital technologies as an impetus for compositionists to pay attention to the visual design of texts (Ball; George; Hocks; Wysocki), it is worth noting that the electronic era of the early 1970s was also a time in composition studies when scholars began to question the privileging of black letters on a white page as the most valued form of discourse.

In addition to highlighting the importance of visual design in print texts, *Montage* also suggests that paying attention to film and television could ultimately help students and teachers invent new ideas for composing alphabetic writing. In explaining why they frequently juxtaposed film scripts and movie stills with more conventional printed texts, Sparke and McKowen note that teachers should strive to make students aware of the ways art forms influence one another, suggesting that teachers engage students in exploring how "Chagall may have paved the way for our understanding of montage in movies, but TV in turn may have made novels such as Ulysses more understandable . . . Newer 'non' books [such as the Montage textbook] may have been influenced by quick cuts on

TV" (*Teacher's Manual* 49). Indeed, the very title of the textbook, *Montage*, represents a way to resee the process of writing through a cinematic term. Whereas film theorists and practitioners such as Eisenstein and Vertov used the term montage to refer to the ways that new concepts could be created through the dialectical juxtaposition of conflicting moving images, Sparke and McKowen employ the notion of montage to name a process of invention that could guide the production of alphabetic texts.

At the current moment when numerous compositionists are experimenting with incorporating still- and moving-image production into our courses, it can be instructive to revisit Sparke and McKowen's attempt to reconceptualize writing in terms of montage theory. Rather than seeing images as purely illustrative of words, Sparke and McKowen remind us that the dialectical tensions between and among images and words can provoke new insights. Challenging the notion that we should focus solely on teaching students to use images to make linear, "coherent" arguments, Sparke and McKowen encourage us to engage students in employing the juxtaposition of words and images as a tool of invention.

TRACK 4: COMPOSITION AS ASSEMBLAGE

Although *Montage* may have deviated greatly from the conventions for arranging materials in textbooks, it was still similar to other more conventional composition readers in that it presented a series of materials organized in a bound book. In contrast, Ray Kytle's radical 1972 *Comp Box: A Writing Workshop Approach to Composition* offers students a box of *unbound* photocopied materials as well as an author's guide that explains ways that students might draw upon the materials (cutting, pasting, rearranging, adding, deleting) to make their own texts. Seeking to provide students and teachers with an inventive "multimedia sampling of our culture" (19), Kytle includes photographs, drawings, advertisements, comics, poems, articles from mainstream publications, articles from underground publications, transcribed interviews, and instructions for making films.[4]

Rather than writing conventional papers in response to the materials in the box, Kytle instead suggests that students could draw upon the materials to create an edited anthology, a magazine, a rhetoric text, or a "mixed bag." In creating their own publications (magazines, books, boxes), students could include some of the texts from the box, though they would likely also add some material that they composed themselves. In considering the kinds of texts that students might create to supplement the selections in the box, Kytle proposes that students should be able to choose any modality and medium that they wish: "it might be a page on which visual media heighten or interpret printed media, it might be a collage, it might be a cartoon or comic strip, it might be an original essay or narrative, it might be an edited tape of an interview with accompanying photographs—it might be anything" (Kytle 16–17). In addition to the many kinds of texts enumerated above, Kytle also suggests that students might compose photo essays, films, or multimedia slideshows.

In rejecting the material form of the bound textbook, Kytle ultimately seeks to challenge modes of education that place the student in the role of the passive recipient. Arguing that the bound textbook inherently reinforces the model of the teacher who fills the student with knowledge, Kytle asserts that "if the medium is the message, then the bound textbook—linear, inflexible, static—cannot encourage nonlinear, flexible, and dynamic response. Furthermore, whatever its intrinsic excellence, a bound textbook necessarily forces the student into a passive role. Using a bound book, the student is recipient, not participant; he is audience, not actor" (2). Even though the bound textbook might incorporate texts relevant to students' lives and might experiment with associative models of arrangement, the bound textbook is still ultimately a collection of texts selected and arranged by an expert author. A student might be able to write a critical response to the text, but the student couldn't alter the text in any substantial way beyond perhaps writing or drawing in a few designated blank spaces (as in *Montage*). In contrast, the presentation of a box with *unbound* pages encourages students to actively create their own boxes by cutting up, rearranging, adding to, and deleting materials.

Reinforcing the notion that the *Comp Box* should be treated as a fluid, alterable text, Kytle reminds students and teachers that "the comp box is not a book. It is source material for a book or magazine.

But not mine, yours. Whatever you do, don't treat the comp box with respect. Cut it up, throw parts of it away, rearrange the bits and pieces" (Kytle 77). Further emphasizing the fact that the *Comp Box* should not be treated as a conventional book, Kytle also informs his readers that he instructed the box's designer to organize the selections in a completely random fashion (77). Rather than asking students to figure out the authors' intent in juxtaposing particular items (as *Montage* often did), Kytle seeks to encourage students to rearrange the text to create their own inventive juxtapositions.

In addition to striving to make students active participants in creating knowledge, Kytle also seeks to heighten students' critical awareness of the ways that media texts construct reality. In particular, Kytle suggests that teachers might help students learn to critically analyze news coverage by assigning them to compose "media collages" (39–40). To make a collage, students would first research and photocopy the ways diverse publications represented an event. Once students have gathered a wide variety of photocopied material, Kyle then instructs them that "you can juxtapose articles that present widely different accounts and interpretations; you can juxtapose conflicting and incompatible headlines; you can juxtapose headlines or excerpted passages with incongruous photographs" (40). This collage would then serve as the basis for an introductory essay that analyzes how and *why* the variations in coverage occurred. For Kytle, it is not enough to have students look at media texts and write about them; rather, it is essential that students actually physically transform media texts—through collage—so that they can gain more complex insights about media manipulation. Accentuating this point about how making collaged media can lead to critical insight, Kytle also suggests that students try to compose "a slanted collage of news coverage . . . to illustrate how judicious selection and editing can slant the way an event is perceived" (40). If students go through the process of selecting and editing images to represent an event in a particular way, Kytle surmises that they might be much less likely to see visual images as presenting undistorted truth.

In addition to challenging conventional notions of media objectivity, Kytle's *Comp Box* also offers a radical critique of the composition field's traditional privileging of individual authorship and "original-ity." Although Kytle suggests that students will likely want to create some of their own materials in order to include perspectives not present in the box, he also leaves open the possibility that students might create a new composition based in large part on remixed fragments from the box itself, from other published sources, or from both. In Kytle's view, the act of placing a found image and a found text together was in itself an act of writing to be valued. By drawing very little distinction between the act of arranging found texts and the act of composing "original" words and images, Kytle implicitly suggests that all composing is ultimately a kind of re-mix or assemblage—that the notion of the wholly original, wholly individual text is a myth.

Although Kytle's work offers a strong critique of conventional notions of original authorship, he never specifically addresses the related concerns of copyright and intellectual property; curiously, however, the front matter of the author's guide does include a rather conventional copyright notice, which states "no part of this book may be reproduced or transmitted in any form or by any means . . . without permission in writing by the publisher." Ironically, if students and teachers actually followed the instructions that Kytle gives in the author's guide, they would likely be violating the law. Of course, it seems clear that Aspen Communications (the publisher) was not all that terribly concerned about students remixing the work since they signed off on the guide in which Kytle encourages the practice; furthermore, the people who owned the copyrights to the individual pieces in the box would be un-likely to ever find out about the students' remixed compositions as they would likely only be shared with friends and peers. In contrast, the contemporary rise of digital publication would make it somewhat more likely that a student could receive a "cease and desist letter" imploring him or her to take down a remixed work (Lessig). Although Kytle was able to ignore intellectual property concerns in his teaching of remixed composition, I would sug-gest that contemporary instructors should make discussion of the politics and ethics of intellectual property a central part of their pedagogies (DeVoss and Webb; DeVoss and Porter; Johnson-Eilola and Selber; Rife). Ultimately, in order to be able to productively build upon Kytle's vision of composition as assemblage, we will need to become vocal "fair-use" activists who vigorously defend students' and teachers' right to remix copyrighted materials for the purposes of analysis, parody, and critique (Center, "Code"; Digirhet; DeVoss and Webb; Faden).

Although Kytle's advocacy of composition as assemblage occurred in a very different context than the contemporary digital environment, it is important to remember that we have a long history in our field of questioning the ideal of the original text—a history that predates both the rise of digital technologies and the so-called "social turn" in scholarship. Whereas many contemporary scholars point to computer technologies as contributing to the development of a remix culture (DeVoss and Porter; Johnson-Eilola and Selber; Sorapure), we might remember that the Xerox machine was also a technology that propelled compositionists to reconceptualize writing as visual and alphabetic assemblage. Indeed, McLuhan (writing a few years before Kytle) offered a compelling analysis of the ways the Xerox machine was causing people to question notions of original authorship. After noting the fact that the invention of printing led to the development of copyright and emphasis on writing as individual expression, McLuhan then suggests that

> Xerography—every man's brain picker—heralds the times of instant publishing. Anybody can now become both author and publisher. Take any books on any subject and custom-make your own book by simply xeroxing a chapter from this one, a chapter from that one—instant steal. As new technologies come into play, people are less and less convinced of the importance of self-expression. (McLuhan and Fiore 123)

In many ways, Kytle's *Comp Box* can be considered an inventive attempt to explore how the technology of xerography might change the teaching of writing. After all, Kytle authored his *Comp Box* by making extensive use of Xerox technology, and he seemed to imagine that students would do the same in creating their own anthologies, magazines, rhetoric texts, or mixed bags. In addition to telling the story of the development of the field of computers-and-writing (Hawisher et al.; Inman), we might also begin to tell the story of *xerography and/as writing.*

Although Kytle's belief in the inventive power of xerography may seem dated in the contemporary era of the "paperless" classroom, many of his pedagogical ideas remain strikingly relevant to the current moment. After all, digital technologies greatly increase the possibilities for creating "media collages" and other critical remix compositions. Whereas Kytle's students were limited mostly to remixing printed texts, students today can now download and remix a wide range of audio and videotexts available on the web (Jenkins; Lessig). Rather than just teaching students to write papers analyzing the rhetoric of digital media, Kytle reminds us that students might best learn to critically analyze media if they have the opportunity to *remake it.*

TRACK 5: REPRISE

From 1967 to 1974 we *had* a moment in the field—a moment when many scholars and teachers were rethinking what it meant to teach writing in light of proliferating new media technologies (television, photocopiers, slide projectors, cassette recorders). This sense of "crisis" propelled compositionists to innovate in designing pedagogical materials, course assignments, and theories of composing. For some scholars such as Corbett and Wiener, attention to new media remained mostly a creative hook to engage students in more conventional forms of pedagogy; for others, such as Kytle, new media offered an opportunity to rethink pedagogy in more radical ways. Although this past technological moment was certainly different from our own, I nevertheless would suggest that contemporary digital composition teachers can learn much from critically revisiting the successes, failures, and contradictions of past compositionists' approaches to new media. To this end, I offer here three critical refrains culled from the composition library at the turn of the 1970s—three refrains that might help us productively resee contemporary digital writing pedagogy.

Refrain 1: Multimedia Can Be Used to
Reinscribe Conventional Pedagogies

In order to persuade teachers to consider incorporating new media, it can be helpful to demonstrate that employing a new technology can help them meet their traditional pedagogical goals. Yet, when we remember the ways that new media was sometimes used to support current-traditional, modes pedagogies in the 1970s, we can be encouraged to question what problematic practices may be reinscribed by our contemporary new-media experiments. Too often, advocates of digital pedagogy (myself included) tend to position multimodal composing as inherently progressive. When we incorporate still image, audio, and video production into our classes, we tend to imagine that our technological innovations are necessarily transformative because they seek to make our courses more relevant to the lives of students and because they ask us to rethink what counts as "writing." But, we must pause to question in what ways our new multimodal assignments might also continue to reify old (and perhaps problematic) assumptions. For example, if we assign students to craft an audio public service announcement, we may inadvertently end up suggesting that they make a kind of simplistic thesis-driven argument that ignores the complexities of the issue they are tackling—a kind of canned five-paragraph essay in a new medium. If we assign students to craft an autobiographical digital story (combining voiceover with pictures), we may unwittingly end up encouraging them to compose a kind of simple "what-I-did-on-my-summer-vacation" essay that lacks depth even if it includes numerous compelling images.[5]

Quite simply, we must remember that new technologies and new forms of composing will not in and of themselves transform or improve our teaching of composition. In fact, if we are not careful, we can quite easily employ new technologies in order to reinscribe potentially ineffective pedagogies. Of course, I recognize that numerous "computers-and-writing" scholars have (at least since the early 1990s) been eloquently making the argument that we must be critical of how new educational technologies can be employed in problematic ways (Eldred; Hawisher and Selfe; Selber); nevertheless,

I think this important caution is worth restating and revisiting in the light of much of the enthusiastic discourse that has surrounded discussions of multimodal pedagogy in recent years.

Certainly, there is much value in considering how new media can help us meet our traditional pedagogical goals, but I contend that we should also stay alert to how emerging technologies might encourage us to radically rethink our assumptions about teaching. For example, when Ray Kytle encountered the photocopier, he didn't merely consider ways it could support his current pedagogical practices—perhaps by making it easier for him to create a "reader" of essays for students to use as models. Instead, Kytle asked how the photocopier could help him rethink the very notion of a teacher-selected textbook; he asked how the photocopier might be used to encourage students to participate in developing pedagogical materials; he asked how the photocopier might encourage us to question our traditional valuing of "originality" in student writing. In other words, Kytle employed the new technology of the photocopier as a kind of inventive heuristic to help him reimagine the teaching of composition. And, to this, I say, "Right on."

Whenever we consider incorporating a new technology into our pedagogy, we should use this moment as an occasion to ask again such crucial questions as:

> What is the role of the teacher in the classroom?
> What is the role of the student?
> How do we evaluate the quality of student texts?
> How do we conceptualize such key terms as audience, invention, revision, process, originality, style, editing, and research (to name a few)?
> How might our learning outcomes need to be revised to account for this newer form of writing?

Although I am arguing we should engage these kinds of fundamental questions in response to emerging technologies, I most pointedly don't mean to suggest that we should immediately jump on every technological bandwagon—haphazardly shifting our pedagogies to keep up with the latest digital fads. After all, my central project in this book is to argue that we should value and build upon our multimodal heritage—that we should be wary of valorizing new technologies so much that we forget the useful elements of our past. Ultimately, then, I would suggest that we should view new technologies not as a force that calls us to jettison our heritage, but rather as a force that encourages us to *resee* and *reimagine* our disciplinary past (as I attempt to do here).

Refrain 2: Juxtaposition and Assemblage Are Powerful Composing Strategies

In order to help students generate ideas for writing, we should consider following Sparke, McKowen, and Kytle in encouraging students to collect a wide variety of "found" words and images and then to explore numerous ways of arranging (or juxtaposing) the visual and alphabetic materials that they have gathered. Instead of focusing multimodal composition instruction solely on teaching students how to combine images and words to make coherent, linear arguments, we should also engage students in employing associative juxtaposition as a heuristic strategy for reseeing and reimagining the world in which they live.[6]

Although it certainly is important to teach students how to focus their inquiries and arguments, we should be careful also to allow ample time for students to collect a wide variety of visual and alphabetic materials so they can employ associative juxtaposition as an invention technique. To this end, we might assign students in a course to keep a digital commonplace book (using free visual mapping software such as Prezi.com or free blogging software such as Wordpress.com). In creating their digital commonplace book, students would be encouraged to collect snippets of material (still images, alphabetic quotes, video clips) drawn from a wide variety of print and digital sources. Although students might develop a broad theme or question to guide their collection, they should be encouraged to search widely in gathering their materials—to include samples and snippets that they find intriguing even if they don't initially seem to be all that relevant to the project. Once students have amassed a substantial collection of found words and images, we can then ask them to experiment with composing associative juxtapositions of the words and images they have collected (perhaps making a simple collage with PowerPoint or Prezi). Once students have created their word-and-image collages, we can then ask them to write or audio-record a reflection about the juxtapositions they have created—to consider ways their associative collages might lead them to develop a novel inquiry question or analytical claim that could spur their alphabetic writing.

As we consider possibilities for integrating associative juxtaposition into composition, we might especially explore ways of adapting Kytle's notion of "media collage" to the contemporary digital classroom. In teaching media collage, we could ask students to conduct extensive web and library research into how a particular event was covered in multiple forms of media: online newspapers, blogs, twitter, television, YouTube, and so on. I especially think it useful to assign students to investigate how an event (a war, a summit, the Olympics) has been represented in media outlets from differing countries. Once students have gathered a wide variety of digital samples of coverage (alphabetic quotations, still images, video clips), they can then experiment with arranging their samples into a media collage using free online software such as Prezi.com or Vuvox.com. Following the advice of Kytle, students might compose a collage that attempts to highlight the differences between various news outlets' coverage or they might compose a collage that specifically seeks to offer an ideologically slanted representation of the event. While I believe this kind of digital media collage could potentially be a valuable assignment on its own, I also think it could serve as a robust multimodal invention activity for an alphabetic essay in which students would rhetorically analyze the ways that diverse media outlets strategically select and arrange words, images, and sounds in order to reinforce a particular ideological view of a news event. In this way, the associative practice of media collage could ultimately work to enhance students' ability to compose the kinds of linear analytical essays that are often required in the university.

Refrain 3: We Should Be Skeptical of
Narratives of Technological "Crisis"

Finally, a look back at composition at the turn of the 1970s can remind us to take a critical perspective about utopian and dystopian
narratives of radical technological change. After all, the printed
book did not disappear as Corbett feared and Kytle celebrated.
Some of the generation of children who were "raised on TV" grew
up to be composition teachers who continued teaching linear print
essays; the idea that composition is assemblage is still a somewhat
radical claim debated in the pages of our journals. Certainly, the
teaching of writing has changed a good deal since 1974, but it hasn't
changed exactly in the ways scholars variously predicted, desired,
and feared. With this in mind, let us all remember to be humble in
our claims about what role today's new media will ultimately play
in transforming writing instruction.

When we look back to the turn of the 1970s, we can be reminded that compositionists have a long history of worrying about the
declining significance of alphabetic literacy in the lives of young
people. In analyzing the influence of emerging technologies on
writing pedagogy, turn-of-the-1970s compositionists too often set
up a simplistic binary opposition between an older generation that
valued print literacy and a younger generation that preferred electronic multimedia. In hindsight, of course, these constructions of
generational difference seem somewhat overstated. After all, as the
television generation grew up, they continued to read and to write
many alphabetic texts (both in print, and more recently, online).
Certainly, the cultural production, distribution, and consumption
of alphabetic texts has changed quite a bit in the past forty years,
but the written word remains a powerful form of communication,
and it is likely to remain so in the coming years.

As we analyze the influence of emerging technologies on teaching
writing, then, we should be wary of simplistic tales of generational
divides such as Marc Prensky's popular distinction between younger
"digital natives" and older "digital immigrants." After all, we must
remember that age is but one of many social factors that influence the

ways people employ communication technologies in their everyday lives. Rather than drawing simplistic divisions between young and old, we need to consider more carefully the ways that interlocking structures of race, class, disability, and gender influence individuals' abilities to access digital composing technologies (Banks; Kirtley; Grabill; Moran; C. Selfe; Selber; Slatin).

As we explore ways that emerging technologies are influencing young students' communication practices, we also must remember that simple "material access" to a computer is only a small part of what it takes for a person to develop a robust and critical technology literacy—only a small part of what it takes for a person to be able to effectively use, critique, and ultimately transform emerging digital composing technologies (Banks).[7] For example, even when teachers encounter classes of students who all have material access to relatively new personal laptops (as I often do), they will still likely find that there are great differences in the functional, rhetorical, and critical literacies that students bring to digital forms of composing (Selber). Despite the rise of "participatory culture" online (Jenkins), I still often encounter many young students who have never made a digital video, never posted a comment on a blog, never played an online game. Despite the proliferation of digital reading and writing technologies, I still encounter numerous young students who prefer to handwrite rough drafts and invention notes, who prefer to read extended text in print rather than online, who prefer to read alphabetic articles rather than watch online videos. Rather than painting all young students with the same broad brush, we instead need to make time to have robust conversations with our students about the diverse ways they *do* and *do not* employ technologies (both analog and digital) in their everyday lives.

In order to engage students in reflecting critically about the politics of technology and literacy, we might ask them to write literacy narratives in which they analyze the role that diverse technologies have played in shaping their communication practices (Kitalong et al.). We might also assign students to research and compose video documentaries in which they interview their peers about the ways diverse technologies are influencing their lives. By asking students to conduct research about the complex and diverse ways that their peers are using and transforming communication technologies, we might ultimately help them come to complicate and challenge the often overly simplistic narratives that have been used to characterize the so-called "digital generation."

4

Zooming Out: Notes toward a History of "Cameras-and-Writing" (1971–84)

WHEN I FIRST STARTED TEACHING COMPOSITION in a computer-lab environment, I was a bit nervous about the hulking machines lurking in my classroom. I worried that I didn't have the technical and pedagogical skills that I needed to integrate these computers in a meaningful way; I worried about how I would respond if students encountered technical difficulties. But, even though I had some concerns, I was heartened by the fact that there was a substantial heritage of computer-based composition pedagogy both at my university and within my broader field—heartened that I could draw upon the collective wisdom of the many "computers-and-writing" teachers who had come before me. When I searched for pedagogical advice in journals such as *Computers and Composition*, I found a wealth of helpful articles from the 1980s and 1990s that detailed productive and nuanced ways that teachers could employ word processors, discussion boards, synchronous chats, hypertext authoring programs, and a whole range of computer technologies to help students improve their ability to compose alphabetic texts. Indeed, I soon found out that the subfield of "computers-and-writing" was so well established that scholars had already begun to write histories of it, tracing compositionists' engagement with computer technologies all the way back to 1979 (Hawisher, LeBlanc, Moran, and Selfe). Although I may personally have had some worries about how well I would be able to integrate networked PCs into my teaching, I still had no question that the computer had a role to play in composition pedagogy—no question that learning how to critically engage computer technologies was an important facet of my professionalization as a composition teacher and scholar.

In contrast, when I first started to teach students to compose visual texts *with cameras*, I felt like I was embarking on some kind of radical, new experiment—an experiment that filled me with a complex mix of exhilaration and doubt. Because my turn to teaching photography provoked such strong, conflicting emotions, I can still remember vividly that first day when I brought digital cameras to my composition class. As I wheeled the cameras into the lab on a cart at the beginning of a two-hour class session, I could feel the atmosphere in the room change; we had been working with desktop computers all term, but this introduction of mobile cameras felt different somehow. After making a few opening remarks about the rhetoric of photography, I briefly showed students how to use the cameras and then I sent groups of students outside of class for fifteen minutes to shoot images of campus. When the students came back to class, I showed them how to edit their images in Photoshop (how to crop, how to filter, how to layer). I then asked students to select and edit a couple of images in order to make us see the campus in a new or unexpected light. As students shared their images toward the end of class, we had a lively and nuanced discussion about how the they had strategically employed framing, camera angle, camera distance, lighting, and contrast in order to construct a particular visual argument about the university.

As a teacher, I was initially very pleased with how this camera activity had motivated students to think more complexly and deeply about visual rhetoric. As I walked home from class, however, my initial enthusiasm began to morph into doubt and concern. Sure, my camera activity had taught students to think critically about photography, but what had they learned about *writing*? After all, I was teaching a composition class in the English department, not a photography class in the art department. I had been well trained to teach writing with computers, but what did I really know about teaching image making with cameras? While I used word-processing software and online databases every day in my work as an English graduate student, I rarely ever had occasion to take photographs or record video for academic purposes. When I reflected about my woeful inexperience with visual composing, I started to worry that my turn to the camera had been *too* innovative—that I was exceeding the bounds of my expertise and responsibility as a compositionist.

Strongly feeling the need to try to connect my camera experiments to past work in composition studies, I began combing through composition scholarship from the 1970s and 1980s looking for moments when past compositionists engaged the arts of photography and filmmaking. As I did this rereading, I came to recognize that the integration of cameras into writing pedagogy was not in fact as new or radical as I had initially thought. Indeed, numerous compositionists in the 1970s and 1980s had sought to integrate analog cameras into the writing classroom—powerfully attempting to help students draw connections between the related arts of writing, filmmaking, and photography. As I searched through the work of these past "cameras-and-writing" scholars, I began to discover a wealth of pedagogical advice about how I could employ photography as a method for enhancing students' invention of alphabetic texts (Kligerman; D. Murray); about how I could engage students in exploring the similarities and the differences in alphabetic and cinematic composing processes (Comprone; Costanzo); about how I could harness video making as a tool to help students become more critical of the ideological manipulations of mass media (Shor). In other words, I began to recognize that my contemporary experiments with cameras-and-writing pedagogy were in fact part of a longer tradition—that I could learn much by revisiting the ways compositionists of the 1970s and 1980s had sought to draw connections between alphabetic and visual composing technologies.

Of course, it is not surprising that I initially failed to recognize how the camera had historically played an important (if limited) role in the disciplinary heritage of composition studies. After all, while the history of writing teachers' engagement with computers has been well documented in the field (Gerard; Hawisher, LeBlanc, Moran and Selfe; Inman; Moran, "Computers"), the history of compositionists' past engagements with cameras has been largely forgotten. Even when scholars have analyzed the historical role of the visual in composition studies, they have generally focused on critiquing past compositionists for failing to attend to cameras and other visual composing technologies

(George; Rice). For example, Diana George concludes her history of the visual in composition by noting that "the history I have outlined clearly links words to high culture and the visual to low, words to production and images to consumption. And yet, as Cynthia Selfe has suggested, teachers of English composition have not, until very recently, had the means to produce communication that went very far beyond the printed word" (31). While George offers a powerful and important discussion of the reasons that many past compositionists tended to marginalize the visual, she also problematically reinforces the common notion that compositionists have little historical experience engaging visual composing technologies such as cameras.

In an attempt to complicate George's historical narrative, then, I offer here four tracks that sample "cameras-and-writing" pedagogies from the 1970s and 1980s—four tracks in which composition scholars powerfully articulate the crucial interconnections between composing with words and composing with images. In track 1, "Writing with Light," I look closely at Donald Murray's and Jack Kligerman's discussions of the similarities between alphabetic and photographic composing processes. In particular, I highlight ways that both Murray and Kligerman suggest that exploration of photography can help students develop a heightened understanding of the importance of "point of view" in alphabetic composing. Placing Murray's and Kligerman's work in dialogue with feminist standpoint epistemology (Haraway), I conclude by demonstrating how expressivist camera pedagogies might be productively extended to address social and political concerns.

In track 2, "Shooting Composition," I revisit the debate occasioned by Richard Williamson's provocative 1971 *CCC* article, "The Case for Filmmaking as English Composition"—a debate that strongly resonates with current arguments about the role of digital video in the composition classroom. Offering a critical synthesis of the perspectives of all the authors involved in the filmmaking debate (Angell; Comprone; Williamson), I ultimately suggest that we should develop complex multimodal pedagogies that attend closely to both the similarities *and* the differences between composing with moving images and composing with words.

In track 3, "Filming Berthoff," I look closely at William Costanzo's 1984 textbook, *Double Exposure: Composing through Writing
and Film*—a textbook that builds upon Ann Berthoff's multimodal
theory of imagination in order to help students learn to draw connections between alphabetic writing and filmmaking. In particular, I
elucidate how Costanzo's work productively demonstrates ways that
experience with filmmaking can help students develop potentially
transferable understandings of invention, arrangement, and style
that they can then apply (and adapt) to alphabetic writing.

In track 4, "Remaking Television," I look closely at Ira Shor's 1980
Critical Teaching and Everyday Life, focusing especially on his discussion of how video composing activities can contribute to students'
development of critical consciousness of the ideological manipulations of television media. Ultimately, I seek to demonstrate that
Shor's *Critical Teaching* offers a powerful and timely pedagogical
vision for how students and teachers might collaboratively employ
video production as a way to uncover and attempt to transform
unjust power structures.

TRACK 1: WRITING WITH LIGHT

While the later tracks in this chapter recover the work of compositionists who actively engaged students in composing visual texts
with cameras, this opening track focuses on composition teachers
who employed photography mostly as an intriguing metaphor (or
optional activity) for enhancing the invention of alphabetic texts.
By uncovering the ways the camera has functioned as a metaphor in
process-based, expressivist writing pedagogies, I seek to demonstrate
that consideration of photography has long played a role in broad
disciplinary imagination of composition—even in pedagogical situations where cameras were not always *physically* present.

I begin this recovery project by looking closely at Donald Murray's
exploration of cameras in his 1984 *Write to Learn*—a textbook that
vividly draws students' attention to considering the similarities between photography (writing with light) and alphabetic composition
(writing with words). In one particularly striking articulation of the
interrelationship between alphabetic and photographic composing,

Murray instructs the composition student to *become* a camera: "go to one spot and sit for an hour and just write down the details that you see. . . . Make yourself a camera that is recording what it sees. Later you can edit the film to find out what it means. . . . It is easy to collect a hundred, two hundred, sometimes many more specifics than that in an hour. You will see what you haven't seen before and make connections that you haven't made before" (30–31). In this quote, Murray evinces a profoundly visual and *photographic* understanding of invention. Invention is not just a process of looking within the individual's psyche; invention is literally a process of *looking outside* the self. By heightening visual awareness, the student can become inspired to write engaging prose that makes his or her reader see the world anew. Yet, Murray not only suggests that seeing can inspire writing; he also argues that writing can inspire seeing. Through the act of writing down visual perceptions (recording the visual in alphabetic words), students might come to see what they "haven't seen before." In asserting that writing down visual impressions can enable the student to "become a camera," Murray implicitly demonstrates that writing is ultimately a *technology of seeing*. The pen is the lens; the paper is the film; the writer is the camera.

Murray's metaphorical instruction to "become a camera" establishes an important foundation for a multimodal composition pedagogy: it suggests that the composition teachers are ultimately in the business of teaching students how to manipulate—how to make use of—technologies of vision. Yet, by keeping the "camera" in the realm of metaphor, Murray implicitly privileges the alphabetic over other modalities. He puts writing teachers in the business of teaching students to analyze visioning technologies but stops short of actually suggesting that writing teachers *literally* ask their students to "become cameras" or even necessarily to "use cameras."

In our current moment, however, the notion of students "becoming cameras" is quickly moving from the realm of fanciful metaphor to the realm of embodied reality. As Donna Haraway argues, we increasingly live in an age in which we are all "hybrids of machine and organism; in short, we are all cyborgs" (151). The distinctions between the eye and the lens, the paper and digital memory card, the letter and the pixel are increasingly breaking down as digital photographic technologies begin to permeate many of our lives. Many students have already literally "become cameras"; they see the world and remember what they see at least in part by taking, circulating, and editing digital images. Yet, even though some students have "become cameras" (have blurred the distinction between lens and eye, human memory and digital pixel), they have not necessarily become *the kinds of* cameras Murray asks them to be. Indeed, many students quickly shoot a still image or a video clip of what most stands out to them and then rapidly circulate that still image or video clip to others. In contrast, Murray's metaphoric "camera" exercise aims to encourage composers to look carefully and extensively—to come to notice aspects of the visual world that they often overlook. Murray asks composers to prolong the invention process (to record without editing) so that they can enhance their options for inventing strikingly original and compelling compositions out of the myriad visual details they collect.

In other words, Murray's camera exercise—his attempt to influence how students use visual technologies for invention—is still highly relevant to an age in which many students have always already been cameras. Instead of asking students to "pretend" to be a camera, a cyborg remediation of Murray's exercise asks students to reimagine how they see with/as cameras:

> Go to one spot and record everything you see with a still or video camera. Later you can review the images to find out what they mean . . . It is easy to collect a hundred, two hundred, sometimes many more photos than that in an hour. You will see what you haven't seen before and make connections that you haven't made before.

Once students have collected these hundreds of visual specifics, they would then have many options for making meaning of them. They could review their footage or image collection to look for interesting connections and details that could prompt an alphabetic essay. Students could also digitally edit their images to create visual compositions that highlight unusual connections or overlooked details. The camera exercise could even result in the production of a multimodal text that blends the alphabetic and the visual.

Although Murray's most extensive discussion of cameras occurs in his chapter on collecting sensory details for invention, the metaphor of the camera also reappears when he discusses the necessity of focusing on a particular aspect of a subject. In introducing the idea that writers adopt a particular point of view, Murray asks students to "think of a photographer at a wedding, continually circling the subject, catching the bride with her father, the couple before the clergyman, the shot down the aisle, the cutting of the cake, the bride's mother, the car with the Just Married sign pulling away. Almost every story can be told from a dozen points of view" (Murray 69). Although Murray points out that finding a point of view can be a wholly mental process, he also suggests that it can be especially helpful to physically go to a place and literally look at it from different angles and distances (70). Just as a photo is framed by the embodied location from which the photographer took it, the page too is framed by the embodied location from which the author wrote it. By connecting alphabetic writing to photography, Murray ultimately suggests that alphabetic writing is a visual-kinesthetic art—an art that requires its practitioners to constantly shift the embodied positions from which they see.

Similarly engaging the connections between photography and writing, Jack Kligerman's 1977 *CCC* article, "Photography, Perception, and Composition," offers a series of pedagogical activities in which students explore the crucial role of "point of view" in both visual and alphabetic composing. Addressing the material reality that many of his students did not have access to cameras, Kligerman suggests that students can simulate the embodied act of taking pictures by creating a viewfinder out of an alphabetic note card:

> I have my students take a small notecard and cut a rectangle out of the center, roughly about the size of a viewfinder of a 35mm camera. Through this little aperture, they must simultaneously choose a scene to write about and locate themselves in space. The rectangle frames experience, minimally composes its elements, and sets up a subject for discussion. But one must look at oneself as well as the objects in the "viewfinder" and consider why one is *there* and nowhere else and what one is

feeling and what one is thinking. Why has this place been
chosen and no other? Thus one learns the meaning of point
of view experientially. (174–75)

Once students have experientially understood the embodied nature
of point of view in photographic composition, they can come to
realize that an alphabetic writer's point of view is also always constrained by his or her embodied location. Even before the student
cuts a hole in the note card and looks through it, the note card has
always already been a technology of framing experience. When the
writer of a research paper records quotes from secondary sources
on a note card, he or she is using the note card as a way of selecting—of *framing*—elements of the source text. Just as the limited
frame of the viewfinder compels the photographer to consciously
select some visual details over others, the small size of the note card
encourages the researcher to consciously select what details he or
she is going to write down. Although visual framing as a concept
is more conventionally associated with photographic technologies,
the note card viewfinder reminds us that the conventional tools of
alphabetic composition (8½' × 11" paper, note cards) are also technologies of visual framing—technologies that constrain the visual
symbols that can be placed within them.

By repurposing a conventional alphabetic technology (the note
card) to function as a tool of photographic production (a viewfinder),
Kligerman implicitly argues for a vision of composition pedagogy
in which students learn to draw connections between alphabetic
and visual composing technologies. Indeed, even when Kligerman
discusses assignments in which students would use actual cameras
to compose photographic essays, he argues "that any exercise in photography should be paralleled by having students write descriptions
of what the photographs represent and what they contain" (177).
Challenging the notion that photography and writing are wholly
separate arts, Kligerman emphasizes that the camera (not unlike the
note card) can be a tool for generating ideas for alphabetic texts. Furthermore, Kligerman usefully asserts that the experience of taking
photographs can potentially help students gain insight into aspects

of the alphabetic writing process—such as point of view—that are often quite abstract and difficult to grasp.

Interestingly, Murray's and Kligerman's discussions of point of view as embodied vision bear a certain affinity with the theories of feminist standpoint epistemologists (Haraway; Harding). For example, Donna Haraway argues that feminists should "insist on the embodied nature of all vision, and so reclaim the sensory system that has been used to signify a leap out of the marked body and into the conquering gaze from nowhere. This is the gaze that mythically inscribes all the marked bodies, that makes the unmarked category [white men] claim the power to see and not be seen, to represent while escaping representation" (188). For Haraway, reclaiming the embodied nature of vision is a way to reject patriarchal, Eurocentric notions of objectivity; to understand vision as embodied (rather than as transcendent and objective) ultimately entails recognizing that we all see the world from particular locations influenced by race, class, gender, and other social categories. Although Murray and Kligerman share with Haraway a commitment to recognizing vision and knowledge making as embodied, it is important to note (not surprisingly) that they problematically depart from her feminist epistemology by casting the knowledge-making body as an individual person "unmarked" by race, class, and gender. In other words, Murray and Kligerman fail to consider how hierarchical social structures (sexism, racism, classism, heteronormativity, ableism) constrain which embodied knowledges are privileged and which are marginalized.

Although Murray and Kligerman neglect to account for issues of power in their discussions of teaching point of view, I still contend that their camera-based activities might be productively revised and extended in order to contribute to feminist pedagogies. After all, Murray's and Kligerman's camera exercises offer powerful kinesthetic ways for us to ask students to consciously engage in acts of embodied vision—to resist adopting the gaze from nowhere. Once students have begun to understand how their physical location influences how they see and represent reality, we may then be able to challenge them to consider how their *social location* also influences their visioning and knowledge-making practices.

Although I recognize that Murray's and Kligerman's discussions of cameras are both politically and technologically "outdated" in some ways, I nevertheless believe that their work still has much to offer contemporary multimodal teachers. Resisting the common notion that alphabetic writing and photography are entirely separate modes of communication, Murray and Kligerman powerfully assert that pens, keyboards, and cameras are all embodied technologies of vision that enable us to notice and record visual, sensory details. Challenging the tendency to see visual composing as a new fad in composition, Murray and Kligerman usefully remind us that compositionists have long been encouraging students to expand the perspectives from which they visually see the world; thus, the current move towards incorporating digital photography into composition is really an extension of a longstanding tradition rather than a radical shift in professional mission.

TRACK 2: SHOOTING COMPOSITION

Although Murray and Kligerman usefully highlight the intersections of photography and writing, they also tend to assign the camera a rather marginal role in composition pedagogy. In contrast, Richard Williamson's 1971 essay in *CCC*, "The Case for Filmmaking as English Composition," offers a radical—and deeply controversial—argument that filmmaking should come to replace much of the alphabetic writing in the composition class. Seeking to develop a pedagogy uniquely adapted to the communication preferences of students at the turn of the 1970s, Williamson asserts that compositionists must account for the reality that the "Woodstock nation, as the young counter-culture has been called, receives its information largely from underground radio, from television, and from cinema" (134). In addition to noting young people's increasing consumption of electronic media, Williamson also points out that many young people were beginning to produce their own media—to wrest control of the moving image away from the corporate television producers and the Hollywood studio system.

In Williamson's view, both universities and Hollywood studios were becoming irrelevant to a generation of young people who increasingly wanted to *produce knowledge* rather than just receive knowledge, to *make media* rather than just consume media:

> In the schools, the students throw rocks at the experts. In Hollywood, the sound stages are empty and the studios sell their property. Those disaffected from the schools are seeking—without much guidance—to express themselves through film and the electronic media, and concurrently young independent filmmakers, defectors from the studios, are filming "on location" across the country. It seems that now is the time to re-direct and combine schools and filmmaking. (136)

Making an argument that sounds eerily similar to those of contemporary advocates of the multimodal turn, Williamson suggests that there is a great disconnect between how students compose in school and how they compose in the rest of their lives. While composition teachers were continuing to ask students to produce alphabetic essays largely for the purposes of evaluation and grading, students were increasingly taking the initiative to compose films outside of school for audiences of their peers.[1]

Seeking to disrupt conventional English pedagogies in which professors lecture to passive students about the correct approaches for interpreting literary texts or the proper formats for writing essays, Williamson argues that incorporating filmmaking into the English composition course could be a way to challenge the status of the English teacher as authoritative expert. In outlining the role of the teacher in an English composition course based on filmmaking, Williamson notes that the teacher "must not be an 'expert' in symbol systems, but must be a 'facilitator' or 'catalyst' in the classroom to respond as an audience to students' 'compositions,' whatever form they might take" (134). For Williamson, the fact that most composition teachers are not experts in filmmaking is ultimately a positive situation because it could lead to the development of more egalitarian classrooms where students and teachers could work together in developing and evaluating cinematic compositions, collaboratively making knowledge about and *with* cinematic media.

Although Williamson's argument for incorporating filmmaking into composition is certainly quite radical, he nevertheless retains a relatively conventional understanding of the composition class as a place where students should learn to develop "clear thought and effective expression" (134). Seeking to demonstrate that his filmmaking-based courses could still ultimately achieve the same objectives as more traditional composition instruction, Williamson asserts that filmmaking could be a way to teach students compositional principles that are transferable across media:

> In a filmmaking class, then, the processes of composition are still dealt with. Only their names have been changed, and this simple act of word magic takes composition out of the mysterious realm of the experts and brings it into the student's own experience. Outlining becomes scriptwriting. Research become shooting. Images and concrete details become shots and takes. Distance and points of view become camera-angles and close-ups. And revising becomes cutting. What is important is that the processes become realer and less esoteric to the student; and even the finished products become significant, something not often said about traditional classroom compositions. (136)

In Williamson's view, filmmaking and alphabetic writing are ultimately quite similar processes. If a student can gain an understanding of the importance of audience, sensory details, or revising in the process of composing a film, the student might then be able to transfer that understanding to his or her alphabetic writing.

Not surprisingly, Williamson's call for incorporating filmmaking into English composition classes provoked a good deal of debate in the pages of *College Composition and Communication*. Beginning the conversation, C. F. Angell offers a substantial critique of how Williamson's article "embodied attitudes harmful to the effective teaching of writing and literature" (256). In Angell's view, the making of a film requires many special cinematic techniques and tools different from those required for alphabetic writing, and thus it does not make sense to claim that the English composition class is the proper place for filmmaking to be taught. Furthermore, Angell suggests that Williamson does "violence to his own discipline" (259) by implicitly arguing that close attention to alphabetic writing skills is no longer necessary in a world of proliferating electronic media. In Angell's response, we can sense at least one of the reasons that Williamson's call for incorporating filmmaking into composition courses went largely unheeded. At a time when compositionists were striving to become recognized for their disciplinary expertise in the teaching of writing, it would ultimately seem too dangerous to turn away from a focus on alphabetic text.

Looking only at Williamson's and Angell's points of view, it would seem that compositionists had only two choices: they could either embrace filmmaking as entirely similar to writing or they could reject it as a wholly different art that should be left to other disciplines. When we look to Joseph Comprone's 1972 response essay, however, we can begin to see a way to mediate between Williamson's and Angell's strident "pro" and "con" positions on the role of filmmaking in the writing class. In Comprone's view, both Williamson and Angell rely on reductive, "either-or" arguments about the interrelationship between film and writing. Challenging the notion that film is either entirely similar to writing *or* entirely different, Comprone argues that compositionists should instead ask the question:

> What are the similarities *and* differences between film and writing and how can they help us compose? Here is where film becomes an invaluable component in a composition pedagogy. Williamson is just not radical enough; he tries to impose the organizing conventions of writing directly on film. Film, however, is most useful precisely because the medium should help us develop fresh compositional perspectives. Often these perspectives derive from the qualitative differences between filmic and written conventions. (56).

By collaboratively attempting to discover the similarities and differences between filmmaking and writing, students and teachers might be able to develop a richer understanding of *both* arts. For example, a student might gain a deeper understanding of the process of composing transitions with words if he or she had to strive to articulate how it was both similar to and different from the process of composing transitions with moving images. Or, a student might be able to rethink options for arranging words if he or she attempted to write an essay *as if* it were a cinematic montage. Or, a student might gain insight into the unique affordances of filmmaking by attempting to translate a print text into a cinematic form and then reflecting about the challenges that he or she encountered. In other words, incorporating filmmaking into composition classes might ultimately help us reimagine how we compose and teach alphabetic writing. If teachers were to continue to maintain the disciplinary separation of English composition and filmmaking, they would fail to gain the insights that "useful film/writing crossfertilization" (58) could provide.

As we once again face a moment wherein we are arguing about what role moving-image production should play in composition, we might usefully heed Comprone's warning to avoid binary, either-or thinking. We can recognize that digital video is playing an increasingly important role in the composing lives of youth *and* that alphabetic text remains an important modality of communication in which many youth engage. We can value the special expertise that film and video scholars bring to teaching video production, while also exploring the unique disciplinary lens that we compositionists can bring to considering the interconnections between video and alphabetic composing. We can ultimately come to see the disciplinary division between filmmaking and writing as a productive space of creative tension—as a space from which it is possible to reinvent models for teaching and practicing multiple modalities of composing.

TRACK 3: FILMING BERTHOFF

As we consider ways that the teaching of film and writing might be usefully combined, we could especially benefit from revisiting William Costanzo's largely forgotten 1984 textbook, *Double Exposure: Composing through Writing and Film*. Although Costanzo's discussion of the technological aspects of film is somewhat dated, his text still offers a very timely discussion of how students and teachers can collaboratively explore both the similarities and differences between alphabetic and cinematic composing. In particular, Costanzo productively outlines a rhetorical pedagogy for integrating alphabetic writing and documentary film production—articulating ways that experience with cinematic composing can potentially help students develop transferable understandings of the rhetorical practices (or canons) of invention, arrangement, and style.[2]

In explaining his theoretical rationale for combining the study of film and writing, Costanzo frequently acknowledges the strong influence of Berthoff—even going so far as to assert in the preface that "a lively image of Ann Berthoff hovered above my desk throughout the writing of this book" (*Double*). In particular, Costanzo credits Berthoff with providing the capacious vision of composing that undergirds his attempt to draw connections between filmmaking and writing: "As Ann Berthoff has reminded us, composing is a matter of making meaning. Whenever people write or read, watch or make a movie, they are combining words, images, ideas and other experiences into meaningful relationships. They are composing in the fullest sense of the term" (169). Drawing on Berthoff's theory of the composing imagination, Costanzo seeks to help students investigate the interconnections between the imaginative acts of viewing, reading, writing, and filmmaking. If students can become conscious of how they actively make meaning when watching a film, Costanzo surmises that they may also become aware of the ways they actively participate in construing and constructing the meaning of alphabetic text. And, similarly, if students can come to understand the value of experimenting with multiple ways of creatively recombining shots in a film, Costanzo hopes that they may also become inspired to consider multiple options for arranging words in the alphabetic texts that they compose.

In addition to adopting Berthoff's capacious definition of composing, Costanzo also follows Berthoff in elucidating the deep connections between elementary education and university composition teaching. Indeed, Costanzo opens the textbook by relating how he first became interested in intersections of film and writing when he found himself teaching first grade in New York City to a group of young students who "were strangers to the universe of print" (1). No-ticing that his first grade students often seemed more at home with the television screen than with the printed book, Costanzo began to consider ways that he might employ moviemaking as a bridge to help students become more engaged in developing alphabetic literacy skills. Using the relatively rudimentary technology of a super 8 film camera, Costanzo collaborated with his first-grade class to produce cinematic versions of the stories in their reading textbook. In the process of making their class film, the first-graders wrote "title cards" and dramatically reenacted scenes based on the alphabetic stories that they had read. Through the activity of translating alphabetic text into film, Costanzo's students developed a much more passionate interest in alphabetic reading and writing than they had exhibited before.

As a result of his positive experience integrating instruction in cin-ematic and alphabetic literacy in the elementary classroom, Costanzo became "impressed by the interrelatedness of seeing, reading, film-ing, writing and those other forms of making meaning which appear actively together in our popular culture but which seemed to be unhappily divorced in most academic settings" (*Double* 2). While Costanzo found the elementary classroom to be a congenial environ-ment for integrating instruction in visual and alphabetic composing, he encountered a very different educational environment when he later began teaching composition in the university setting where

> writing, reading, film study, and "communication skills" are often taught in separate disciplines, usually in different de-partments and in very different ways. Instead of tracing con-tinuities of structure, style, and thought among the media, our older students learn to study them isolation. And this can build certain barriers. The project represented by this book is an effort to break down those barriers. (2)

Challenging the rigid compartmentalization of knowledge in the modern university, Costanzo ultimately argues that the artificial disciplinary division between film and writing instruction in higher education unnecessarily works to prevent students from drawing connections between alphabetic and visual ways of making meaning.

In outlining possible ways to include filmmaking in college composition pedagogy, Costanzo particularly suggests having the class as a whole produce a documentary film as a term-long project that "runs parallel" to other writing assignments (14). In explaining his preference for the documentary genre, Costanzo notes that documentaries (more than fiction films) tend to be composed in ways that are similar to research-based, academic essays. In composing a documentary film, the students must first gather a variety of sources (interviews, footage of places and events) and then consider ways to arrange that footage in order to make a specific argument for a particular audience.

In explaining how a class documentary project can help students understand complex composing processes, Costanzo relates the story of a composition class that collaboratively composed a documentary film about their college. At first, the class set out with super 8 cameras to make a kind of "exposé" of how college bureaucracy harms students—a topic inspired by their difficulties navigating the registration system. As the class began shooting around the college, however, they ended up finding many exciting things happening on campus in art studios, performance spaces, science labs, and student clubs. Because the footage they gathered no longer fit their original argument, the class collectively decided to change their original purpose and audience "to make a movie that would show high school students what the campus had to offer" (16). In this way, the students gained an understanding of the complex, evolving nature of invention—coming to recognize ways they might reinvent their arguments based on the footage they gather, the observations they make, the sources they read, and the words they write. Once students have gained the experience of using composing as a method of reinvention in the medium of filmmaking, they may be more willing to also approach an alphabetic research project as a flexible, adaptable process of discovery.

In telling the story of the class film about the college, Costanzo also highlights the ways that documentary composing can help attune students to the rhetorical process of arrangement:

How to arrange these shots [of the college] was more of a problem. A random sequence might appear tedious, chaotic. One solution was to classify the scenes into groups: one section for academic opportunities, a section for social events, a third for sports. Someone suggested a chronological order, starting with a students' arrival on campus and following her journey through a typical day, using reaction shots of her expressions to link different scenes. Another suggestion was to compare the college's facilities and staff to those of high schools in the area, shifting back and forth to dramatize the contrasts between secondary school and college life. In short, the class proposed most of those organizational strategies that are taught in composition courses. In this case, it wasn't a matter of filling in prescribed formats. The composition's shape and style grew out of the message and the material. (16)

In this way, Costanzo points out that many modes of organization may be transferable across modalities (at least to some extent). In organizing words and/or images, both filmmakers and writers often rely on crafting narratives, setting up contrasting oppositions, or grouping material by topical categories. By considering multiple options for organizing material for a film, students can come to a dynamic rhetorical understanding of how patterns of arrangement can be adapted to audience and purpose. In this way, students can begin to move beyond the tendency—reinforced by conventional modes of discourse pedagogy—to pick one rigid form or organization and stick with it regardless of context. Once students have come to develop a more flexible understanding of arrangement as filmmakers, they may also be more likely to experiment with multiple ways of organizing their essays as well.

In addition to suggesting that students record and then edit their own "original" video material, Costanzo also asserts that students can learn about invention and arrangement by reediting—or remixing—found footage recorded by others. Drawing on the work of avant-garde Soviet filmmakers such as Kuleshov and Eisenstein, Costanzo presents a series of exercises that ask students to create a cinematic montage by creatively recombining footage from existing films. Emphasizing how montage composing can be a tool for fostering invention, Costanzo urges students to "test several arrangements of the same shots. Try matching scenes that seem quite different as well as those that seem alike. Look for unexpected connections that might lead in new directions" (*Double* 119). In asking students to compose cinematic montages, Costanzo ultimately seeks to engage students in considering how invention in both film and writing often arises from the creative recombination of existing materials.

Challenging the idea that making a montage film is radically different from composing an "original" print text, Costanzo reminds students that montage editing

> has much in common with the writing process. Writing at its best is rarely a one-shot deal—no simple question of deciding what to say ahead of time and getting it all down in one single take. Practicing writers produce a lot of chaos, much of it made of memories, fragments of events, other people's words and thoughts. Writing something original is often a matter of editing these borrowed fragments, which means realigning the familiar into unfamiliar forms, noticing relationships, and pursuing them to new ideas. (119)

In many ways, Costanzo hopes that the film-editing process will help make the chaos of invention visible to students; once students have appreciated the value in experimenting with multiple juxtapositions in making a montage, they might also attempt to use montage techniques as a way to reinvent their alphabetic writing.[3] In order to help students draw the connection between cinematic montage and alphabetic invention, Costanzo assigns students to translate a series of film stills into alphabetic sentences and then experiment with multiple ways of arranging those sentences (117–18). By asking students to treat alphabetic sentences as if they were cinematic shots in a montage, Costanzo ultimately hopes to encourage students to move beyond a static, linear understanding of alphabetic composing—to recognize the ways that writers (as well as filmmakers) can gain new insights by radically rearranging their materials.

In addition to exploring how the rhetorical practices of invention and arrangement are similar across media, Costanzo also considers ways that the teaching of style (for example, word choice, sentence structure) might be enhanced by film study. Although Costanzo is acutely conscious of the fact that the syntax of written language and the syntax of film are profoundly different, he nevertheless suggests "that students who get interested in the mechanics of film gain a new respect for all forms of mechanics, which transfers indirectly to their writing" (*Double* 6). In other words, if students can become interested in closely analyzing the implications of the way shots are systematically composed and arranged, they may also become interested in considering the rhetorical nuances of sentence structures. To this end, Costanzo offers activities in which students draw connections between film editing and sentence-level composing (115). As a kind multimodal exercise in *copia*, Costanzo asks students to first explore how many logical ways they can arrange a series of 3 to 4 still images to make meaning. Costanzo then assigns students to translate the visual shots into alphabetic phrases, exploring all the possible ways they could combine those phrases into one sentence. Although Costanzo points out to students that film sequences and alphabetic sentences rely on quite different grammatical structures, he also suggests that there may be some similarities in the rhetorical choices involved in image combining and sentence combining. For example, in both writing and film editing, composers must carefully arrange their words or their shots in order to "emphasize certain details over others" (114). If a student can come to understand how shot order can convey meaning in film composition, the student may then become more attentive to considering the rhetorical effects of word order in alphabetic writing. Rather than suggesting to students that their experiences with viewing and image making are irrelevant to the work of the composition class, Costanzo productively argues that we should help students consider how they might build upon their visual literacies in learning to analyze and to write alphabetic texts.

When we look back at the work of Costanzo, we can be reminded that cinematic composing and alphabetic writing are deeply interrelated arts. If students can gain new insights about the rhetorical practices of invention, arrangement, and style through the process of making a video, they may be able to adapt this knowledge to their writing of print texts. Rather than positioning video composing as a new kind of assignment to be dropped into the last weeks of a composition class, we might instead follow Costanzo in integrating alphabetic and video composing throughout the duration of a course. For example, we might assign students to work over several weeks to compose both an alphabetic paper and a short video on a similar topic. During this process, then, we could engage students in a variety of alphabetic and cinematic techniques for inventing, arranging, and editing their arguments—encouraging students to reflect critically about both the similarities and the differences between composing words and composing moving images. In this way, we could potentially help students to develop a capacious understanding of rhetoric that they could then apply (and adapt) to all the diverse composing technologies and situations they will encounter in their future both in the university and beyond.

TRACK 4: REMAKING TELEVISION

While Costanzo powerfully outlines a robust rhetorical and process-based approach for integrating film and writing instruction, he largely fails to consider the broader political and ideological implications of visual composition pedagogies. Seeking to explore ways that writing teachers might employ video composing to contribute to social change, I turn now (once again) to Ira Shor's foundational *Critical Teaching and Everyday Life* (1980). Articulating the crucial importance of engaging visual media in the composition class, Shor argues that film and television are among the primary cultural formations "at work to produce 'false consciousness,' that is, manipulated action and reflection which leads people to support their own oppression" (55).[4] In other words, popular films and television programs encourage people to view the problems in their lives as wholly individual rather than social—to ignore the ways they can act collectively to challenge social hierarchies of class, race, and gender. In addition to emphasizing how the content of mass media reifies individualist narratives of success, Shor also asserts that mass media produces false consciousness by fostering a culture of "spectatorism"—a culture in which people merely consume but never produce the texts of mass media that so pervade their lives.

In observing the prevalence of mass media spectatorship in the lives of students in the 1970s, Shor notes that students:

> watch television, go to movies, and receive information from corporations and politicians through dramatized advertisements. As an enormous audience for video, radio, magazine, and billboard commercials, they have been socialized into spectating theatrical persuasions. The information flow goes one way, from the medium to the person. Each student is not trained to analyze critically the message thrown at her or him or to be a creator of the media filling daily life. (241–42)

Although politicians and corporations (the ruling elite in the class system) have the ability to shape the messages of television, Shor notes that working-class people and other marginalized groups are positioned solely as media spectators. When people are denied the ability to shape the media that pervade their lives, they lack the tools they need to articulate their interests and collectively organize to challenge social inequalities.

Even though Shor is critical of television media, he realizes that banishing video production from composition would ultimately be counterproductive to his goal of liberatory teaching—that when compositionists ignore media production they reinforce the dominant ideology of spectatorism. Thus, Shor seeks to engage composition students in producing "video plays" about social issues relevant to their everyday lives (197–98; 241–65). In particular, Shor notes that engaging students in video production can help "dissolve the alienation of producers from receivers. For the first time, they experience themselves as artists and as an audience which has shaped the language and images of the medium" (242). Rather than seeing television as an immutable, unchangeable part of everyday life (a transparent representation of reality), students who have the experience of producing video are able to begin to conceptualize television as a medium that has been shaped by particular people for particular ideological ends.

In addition to noting ways that video production can help students come to recognize the ideological manipulations of television, Shor also suggests that the experience of composing video plays can contribute to students' development of "critical consciousness" of the unjust power relations that structure their everyday lives. For example, Shor tells the story of one class that collaboratively developed a project in which they created video plays that sought to critique and reconstruct the traditional practices of schooling:

> A freshman composition class began a long study of traditional and experimental education, based in its own experience of school and its ideas for reconstruction. They wrote criticisms of their prior education, and then broke into work-teams to prepare video scripts that would dramatize their written analysis. They first dramatized the negative old way they were taught and then offered a model of the new classroom relations they wanted, based on egalitarianism and critical modes for study. Blended into the longer segments on old and new education were shorter pieces in mime and dialogue that satirized their authoritarian schooling. (198)

For students, the experience of school is one of embodied interaction between teacher and student; school is not just an idea students think about, it is a reality they see, feel, and hear every day. In order to gain a more holistic sense of how school can be transformed, it makes sense for students to move from the page to the stage—for students to actually enact the ways that the embodied experience of school needs to be changed. In Shor's view (influenced by Freire), the development of critical consciousness is not simply an alphabetic process of renaming the world; it is a multimodal process of reseeing, rehearing, and refeeling the world as well. As a result, students may improve their ability to analyze and challenge oppressive social structures if they have the opportunity to compose video dramas that combine aural, alphabetic, and *visual* ways of knowing.

In teaching students to produce video texts in the 1970s, Shor usually asked them to write a script, rehearse it, and then perform it in front of a camera. Students in Shor's class were able to gain access to video cameras (in a studio) for a limited time, but they did not have access to the equipment needed to edit video. Given these technological limitations, it made sense for Shor to focus on having students create scripted video performances. In the contemporary digital moment, however, many students increasingly have access both to relatively inexpensive mobile technologies for recording video (cell phones, flip cameras, webcams) as well as to free digital software for editing video (Movie Maker on PCs, iMovie on Macs). Whereas students in Shor's classes had to write scripts and perform them in one take in the style of TV drama or comedy, contemporary students might be able record footage in their communities (interviews, events) and then edit the footage to tell a persuasive story in the style of a news program or documentary. When students gain the experience of recording and *editing* documentary footage, they may be able to develop a much more critical sense that television news is not a transparent representation of reality. In making a documentary, students must make choices about what to shoot, whom to interview, what kinds of questions to ask. Once students have selectively gathered all their footage, they then need to figure out how to edit it (cut, rearrange, layer) in order to tell a particular kind of story—to construct a particular version of reality. Once students have made these kinds of conscious decisions about how they are going to (re)present reality in a video documentary, they may be more likely to be critical of any kind of news special or "reality" program they watch—to look for ways that the editing of the program and even the selection of the subjects ultimately reveals an ideological point of view.

In teaching students to compose video texts in the 1970s, Shor ultimately sought to empower them to create representations of reality that contested those offered by mainstream media outlets. Shor noted that students often became so strongly invested in their video production projects that they sought to have their work "broadcast outside the college"—to make their voices heard in the broader public sphere (197). Of course, students in the 1970s faced great hurdles in distributing their video work to a broader public audience; they had to either arrange screenings or convince a television producer to air their work. In contrast, contemporary digital students have the option to publish their work on free digital video-sharing sites such as YouTube, potentially reaching a wide audience both within and beyond their local region.[5] As a result, it is timely that we reclaim and critically extend Shor's vision of the composition class as a place where students can learn to employ video production as a tool for advocating social change.

TRACK 5: REPRISE

In the past four tracks, I have sought to demonstrate that compositionists have a substantial tradition of engaging cameras as composing technologies—a substantial tradition of critically exploring the affinities and tensions between writing, filmmaking, and photography. Just as compositionists have long recognized that the development of the personal computer was a catalyst for reimagining the teaching of writing, we should also remember that the development of the super 8 camera was a historical moment that encouraged compositionists to rethink their work. Rather than defining our field's technological heritage narrowly as being limited to considering the intersections of "computers-and-writing," we might instead come to tell a more expansive historical narrative about how compositionists have engaged a wide diversity of analog and digital technologies for composing with words, images, and sounds.[6]

*Refrain 1: Photography Can Be a Powerful Tool
for (Re)Inventing Alphabetic Texts*
When we look back to the work of Donald Murray and Jack Kligerman, we can be reminded that there are useful connections to be drawn between alphabetic and photographic composing processes. Whether they are writing with words or writing with light, students must work to develop a unique "point of view" on their subject— to emphasize some details and concerns while excluding others. Whether they are taking a photograph or writing an academic essay, students must carefully consider how their embodied location influences what they are able to see. Because photography is an art that many of our students already practice on a regular basis, it makes

sense for us to help them consider how they might build upon their camera literacies in inventing and revising alphabetic texts.[7]

In many cases, the students in our classes are already making rhetorical choices about how to compose photographs in order to represent their identities to diverse audiences (using social networks such as Facebook and Flickr). As a result, it makes sense for teachers to help students consider ways that they might employ photography in order to invent ideas for autobiographical writing. For example, we might ask students to draw upon their personal photo archives in order to create a visual slideshow that tells the story of how they came to develop a particular identity or belief about the world. Once students have composed their slideshows, they can they write an informal reflection in which they discuss why they selected the photos that they did—critically considering what their photo story both reveals and conceals about them. Through the process of selecting, arranging, and writing reflectively about personal photos, students might generate useful questions and ideas for a critical autobiographical essay in which they explore how a particular aspect of their identity or worldview has been socially and rhetorically constructed over time. By offering students a range of visual and alphabetic options for critically reseeing and reimagining their lives, we might be able to help them to move beyond simple clichés and generalizations to develop more vivid and nuanced personal narratives.

In addition to engaging students in drawing upon their photo archives to craft personal narratives, we also might ask students to employ cameras as tools for pursuing research and advocacy about local social and political issues. For example, students might take photographs of inaccessible building entrances and rooms on their campus—using photography as a medium to persuasively document and attempt to challenge the ableism embedded in the university architecture. Or, students might take contrasting photographs of the produce available at their local grocery store and at their local farmers' market—highlighting the fact that conventional grocery stores often feature many "out-of-season" items that have been transported thousands of miles using fossil fuels. Once students have employed photography as a tool for researching and documenting a local civic issue, we could then ask them to write an alphabetic essay in which they offer further evidence to support and/or complicate the arguments they made in their photos. By engaging students in reseeing their communities with both photographic and alphabetic tools, we might be able help them develop critical insights about civic issues they would not have discovered through the written word alone.

Refrain 2: Alphabetic and Cinematic Composing Are Dynamically Interrelated Arts

Rather than positioning film and writing as either inherently similar or inherently distinct arts, we might instead follow Comprone and Costanzo in developing complex pedagogies that offer students a recursive "double exposure to the collaborative powers of the written word and the visual image" (Costanzo i). One the one hand, this kind of "double exposure" to film and writing can potentially lead students to discover some rhetorical and process-based principles that they can apply (and adapt) to both alphabetic and cinematic forms of composing. Yet, on the other hand, this pedagogy of "double exposure" can also help students learn to reflect about the unique affordances and limitations of alphabetic and visual composing technologies—to reflect about how they will likely need to adapt or rethink some of their composing strategies whenever they begin working in a new medium.[8]

In order to help students critically investigate the similarities and differences between alphabetic and cinematic composing, it makes sense for teachers to consider ways that they can engage students in recursively practicing the arts of filmmaking and writing at the same time. To this end, teachers might create an assignment sequence in which students simultaneously work to compose both an alphabetic essay and a documentary video about an issue, a cultural phenomenon, an organization, or a place in their local community. While Costanzo suggests having the whole class make a documentary film together, I must note that I personally find it much more pedagogically manageable to have individual students or small groups working on different—though perhaps related—projects.

Using both cameras and alphabetic writing tools, students would ideally spend several weeks gathering a wide range of visual and alphabetic materials about their chosen subject. For example, in the process of conducting research, students might go to a local place one day and record video footage; they might then return to the same place on another day and take alphabetic field notes. Similarly, students might conduct some interviews with a video recorder, while they might conduct other interviews using text-based chat (or e-mail). As students experiment with employing both visual and alphabetic methods of invention, teachers could engage them in reflective discussion about how both alphabetic writing and filmmaking entail an intensive recursive process of generating and rearranging copious amounts of material. Just as successful documentary filmmakers often shoot a hundred times more footage than they include in the final cut, so too do successful academic writers consult many more sources and write many words than ultimately appear in the final manuscript. Furthermore, just as documentary filmmakers often discover new arguments in the process of gathering and arranging their footage, so too do successful writers recognize that composing can be a way of reseeing or reimaging their preexisting conceptions about an issue. After highlighting these broad similarities in alphabetic and cinematic invention processes, teachers can then move to asking students to reflect about the unique affordances and limitations of diverse alphabetic and visual technologies of invention. For example, as students begin to review their collection of video footage and alphabetic notes, we can ask them to write reflections in which they discuss the ways that the technologies of the camera, the pen, and the keyboard all differently influenced what they were able to *see* about their subject.

After students have gathered and generated a wide variety of words, images, and sounds, they can then turn their attention to the process of selecting, arranging, and revising their material to craft both an alphabetic essay (four to six pages) and a short video (two to three minutes). As students begin shaping their material in both alphabetic and cinematic compositions, teachers will likely want to engage them in reflective conversations about how writing and video composing ultimately rely upon quite distinct temporal and spatial logics. While word processors enable students to arrange text linearly within the conceptual space of the "page," video editors enable students to simultaneously layer words, images, and sounds on the space of a "timeline." Because word processors and video editors present such strikingly different interfaces for organizing material, it is highly unlikely that students will be able to seamlessly apply the exact organizational structure they used for a paper in order to guide their arrangement of a video on the same topic. Rather, students will need to consider how the unique affordances and limitations of video editors may lead them to rethink how they are arranging their argument (or perhaps even to adopt a new argument entirely).[9]

As a way to help students critically reflect about the similarities and differences in how print texts and videos make arguments, we can engage them in collaboratively creating a rubric for evaluating the rhetorical effectiveness of the videos that they make. In facilitating this process, teachers can encourage students to develop evaluative criteria that might apply to both print and video composing as well as to create evaluative criteria that are medium specific. So, for example, a class might decide that "clear sense of audience" applies to both forms of composition, while the criterion "soundtrack complements the emotional tone of the words" is specific to video. In this way, students could potentially develop a robust understanding of the possibilities and the limitations of transferring rhetorical principles and criteria from one medium to another.

Refrain 3: Media Critique and Media Production Are Symbiotic Activities

As cultural studies pedagogies have come to prominence in the past fifteen years, it has become increasingly common for compositionists to engage students in writing critical alphabetic essays about popular visual and multimodal texts; nevertheless, it remains relatively rare for compositionists to teach students to *produce* visual and multimodal texts themselves. Yet, if we turn back to the critical pedagogy of Ira Shor, we can be reminded that the teaching of media analysis and the teaching of media production are deeply interconnected activities. In particular, Shor's work productively suggests that experience with video production can ultimately help students to become more critical of the ways that multimedia texts construct versions of reality that support particular ideological points of view.

In the 1970s, Shor focused on engaging students in producing video dramas and news programs as a way of helping them learn to critically analyze and attempt to transform the medium of television. Although I see value in these activities, I will focus here on discussing how Shor's work might be extended to address the proliferation of online video sharing sites such as YouTube. Offering new possibilities for employing video to teach critical media analysis, websites such as YouTube and Hulu make available a wide variety of television and film content. Not only can teachers ask students to watch and analyze this video content, they can also engage students in editing and remixing it. (In order to make a video remix, students would need to download the video using free software such as zamzar.com, and then import the footage into a video editor such as iMovie.) By engaging students in remixing media videos, we may ultimately be able to help them develop a more robust critical understanding of how news outlets often strategically edit footage in order to make a particular argument.

As a way to help students employ video remix as a critical invention activity, we can assign them to reedit a video of a political speech downloaded from a site such as YouTube, C-Span, or Americanrhetoric.com. To guide students' remixing process, teachers can ask them to edit their selected speech in order to pursue one or more of the following rhetorical goals:

- persuading an audience to view the speech a new way, noticing aspects of the speech that would often be overlooked;
- making the speech appealing to an audience different from the one for which it was intended;
- offering a critique or parody of the arguments and perspectives of the political orator that the student is remixing.

In some cases, students might perform a relatively judicious remix in which they simply choose to highlight some aspects of the speech over others, perhaps by making a collection of those moments in the speech that they think would be most likely to appeal to young college students. In other cases, students might radically reedit the speech to make it convey a message different from what the rhetor likely intended, perhaps by cutting up and rearranging the speaker's sentences to make it appear as if he was agreeing with the critiques of his strongest opponents. By going through this process of editing a speech to convey a particular rhetorical point, students can potentially develop a stronger critical literacy about how news organizations often selectively edit political speeches and events to reinforce a particular ideological outlook (Dubisar and Palmeri).

In addition to asking students reedit political oratory, we also might engage them in making more complex remix videos in which they assemble and juxtapose clips from a range of sources to offer a critical analysis of a cultural phenomenon. For example, a student might create a remix that juxtaposes proclamations of a "postracial" era with snippets of the many racist comments that persist in contemporary political discourse—persuasively refuting the common ideological trope that the mere election of Barack Obama undid centuries of material racial oppression. [10] Or, a student might create a collection of clips that highlight the prevalence of negative discussions of body image among female characters in teen movies—arguing that Hollywood media often works to reinforce sexist beauty standards that oppress women. In many cases, the process of composing these kinds of remixes will encourage students to pay close attention to the rhetorical and ideological implications of visual texts; as a result, video remix composing might come to serve as powerful invention activity that could help students generate ideas for a critical alphabetic essay about a cultural phenomenon. [11]

Finally, I think it important to note that video production has potential to be a powerful way for students to advocate for the kinds of social change that they would like to see in the world. By composing and distributing persuasive videos to sites such as YouTube, students can potentially make their voices heard to audiences well beyond the immediate classroom. For example, one of the students in my 2008 first-year seminar "Political Rhetoric and

New Media" produced a parodic video remix of Sarah Palin that has to date received over 120,000 views on YouTube (Kostyosj). In many cases, students are already avid viewers of online video, and thus they may already have a keen sense of what kind of rhetorical strategies are most likely to be persuasive to the YouTube audience; furthermore, because many students see themselves as part of the audience for online video, they are often quite willing and able to provide rigorous and helpful critiques of the persuasive videos of their peers. Ultimately, if we wish to teach students to employ rhetoric as a tool for advocating for social change, then it makes sense to engage them in composing the kinds of persuasive digital video texts they often strongly value.

Epilogue

THROUGHOUT THIS BOOK, I HAVE ATTEMPTED to demonstrate that compositionists have a rich multimodal heritage that we can build upon in order to reimagine contemporary pedagogical practices. But I remain very conscious that the discipline of composition studies is a deeply and complexly situated one—that there is great diversity in the student bodies we engage, the institutional contexts in which we work, the physical environments in which we teach, and the theoretical frameworks on which we draw (Ede). As a result, it is ultimately impossible for any single book to offer a detailed vision of multimodal curricular transformation that can be applied in all the diverse locations where compositionists can be found. Nevertheless, I would like to conclude here by outlining three broad pedagogical goals that we might all attempt to pursue in diverse and modest ways in our work in first-year composition programs, in writing-across-the-curriculum initiatives, in undergraduate writing majors, and in graduate programs.

GOAL 1: DEVELOP FLEXIBLE, MULTIMODAL STRATEGIES FOR INVENTING AND REVISING ALPHABETIC WRITING

When we look back to the work of Elbow, Flower and Hayes, Berthoff, and others, we can be reminded that multisensory imagery and spoken conversation play a crucial role in the alphabetic writing process. As a result, it makes sense for composition teachers to engage students in informal auditory and visual composing activities as a way to help them invent and revise alphabetic texts. To this end, first-year writing faculty might consider integrating one low-stakes multimodal activity into every alphabetic writing assignment sequence in the course. In some cases, teachers might explore how students could use digital audio recording, digital image collage, and digital photography to resee or rehear their writing; however, it is important to note that digital technologies are not necessarily required for a robust multimodal writing pedagogy (Shipka, "A Multimodal"). As Patricia Dunn has compellingly demonstrated, teachers can engage students in powerful multimodal invention activities using such "old" technologies as pen, paper, and the human body itself—reimagining writing by drawing images on paper and by engaging in live performance in class.

Early on in the composition course, teachers might require that students complete a particular kind of multimodal invention activity so that they can gain experience with an invention strategy (such as image collage or sketching) that may be new to them. Ultimately, though, the teacher's aim should be to help students reflect critically about the strengths and limitations of various alphabetic, auditory, and visual methods of invention—to help students develop a flexible set of multimodal invention strategies that they can employ and adapt in diverse contexts. To this end, teachers should engage students in regular reflective writing and discussion about multimodal strategies for invention, scaffolding instruction so that students can move from participating in directed multimodal activities to making informed, reflective choices about which auditory, visual, and alphabetic strategies will be most helpful to them.

Extending beyond the borders of first-year writing programs, we compositionists also have a responsibility to work with colleagues in other disciplines to infuse multimodal approaches to teaching and learning throughout the university. As leaders and participants in writing-across-the-curriculum (WAC) initiatives, we should actively resist the common tendency to present alphabetic writing as inherently the best tool for promoting active learning in disciplinary courses; instead, we might develop a more capacious vision of "composing to learn" that emphasizes how the integration of informal writing, speaking, *and* visual-production activities can enhance students' reflective understanding and application of course concepts

(Bridwell-Bowles, Powell, and Choplin). And, as we work to design workshops and institutes about "composing to learn," we should seek to foster a spirit of collaboration across disciplines—recognizing that all faculty in the university have important insights to contribute about how speaking and visual composing activities can enhance student learning. In particular, WAC directors might take inspiration from Berthoff and Emig in developing workshops or institutes that bring together instructors from "allied arts" fields—providing opportunities for teachers of writing, theater, visual art, film, music, graphic design, and architecture to collaboratively develop and share multimodal strategies for promoting creative invention in their disciplines.

In addition to collaboratively reflecting about multimodal pedagogy with our colleagues in the university, I would also suggest that compositionists work to develop and strengthen partnerships with K–12 teachers. After all, we would do well to remember that many of the early proponents of multimodal pedagogy in our field—Berthoff, Smitherman, Emig, Costanzo—were deeply inspired by their work with K–12 teachers and students. Although I will shy short of endorsing Berthoff's proposition that all PhDs in rhetoric "be required to teach third grade for a year" (*Making* 23), I think there is no question that we can learn much about multisensory approaches to writing instruction by engaging in dialogue with teachers of younger students, and I would note that National Writing Project sites would be one particularly fruitful location for these kinds of collaborative conversations to occur.

Finally, if we as a field are to truly honor our commitment to studying and teaching writing as a multimodal process, we must also work to integrate multimodal invention and revision activities into our graduate-level curricula in masters and doctoral programs. Rather than limiting considerations of multimodality to special seminars in "computers-and-writing" or "digital rhetoric," we should also look for ways to integrate informal visual and audio composing into other classes that do not take up the question of technology directly. For example, in a seminar on the history of rhetoric, graduate students might be asked to try out some of the spoken-performance exercises (or *progymnasmata*) that were common in ancient rhetorical instruction; or, in a seminar on feminist rhetoric, students might be encouraged to collaboratively craft a digital audio response to one week's reading; or, in a seminar on research methods, students might gain experience with employing photography as a method of ethnographic observation. Ultimately, if we are to prepare graduate students to study and teach alphabetic writing as a multimodal process, then it is imperative that we offer them numerous curricular opportunities to employ visual and auditory strategies of knowing in order to invent and revise their scholarly writing.

GOAL 2: APPLY AND ADAPT RHETORICAL AND PROCESS-BASED THEORIES TO COMPOSE PERSUASIVE ALPHABETIC, AUDITORY, AND VISUAL TEXTS

When we critically revisit many of the foundational theories of rhetoric and composing process that animated our discipline in the 1960s, 1970s, and 1980s (Berthoff; Corbett; Flower and Hayes; Emig; D. Murray; Smitherman), we can be reminded that we have a substantial heritage of investigating the similarities and differences between alphabetic writing and other modalities of composing. Rather than positioning our field as one narrowly dedicated to teaching students to compose alphabetic texts, we might instead reclaim our heritage as a field dedicated to helping students develop a robust understanding of rhetoric and creative process that they can apply and adapt to all the diverse forms of alphabetic, auditory, and visual composing they are likely to encounter in their lives.

While I recognize that most first-year composition programs will need to continue to place a special emphasis on alphabetic writing instruction, I would suggest that it is reasonable for writing program administrators and faculty to begin transforming curricula to include one formal assignment sequence in which students attempt to "translate" an argument from one modality to another. For example, teachers might ask students to attempt to transform an argument from a live spoken presentation to a piece of writing, or from a print text to an audio essay, or from a video to an alphabetic essay. As students engage in the process of attempting to translate an argument from one modality to another, we can then ask them to reflect critically about the unique affordances and limitations of various forms of composing—preparing them to make informed rhetorical choices about which modalities will best enable them to convey their persuasive arguments. Even if teachers and students do not have access to newer multimedia technologies, they can still potentially investigate composing processes across modalities by making live speeches in class, by crafting photo essays with cell phone cameras, or by composing photo slideshows with PowerPoint. Although I certainly see value in introducing students to newer technologies for audio and video composing, I also think it important to remember that our ultimate goal in the first-year course should not be to teach students to become professional "new media" producers but rather to engage them in reflectively considering how theories of rhetoric and process can travel across modalities.

While the inclusion of informal multimodal invention activities does not necessarily require teachers to undertake a major conceptual shift in their pedagogies, the turn to integrating a more formal multimodal composing assignment sequence often represents a much more challenging transformation for teachers to make. As a result, I would suggest that this kind of curricular change can best be achieved through an evolutionary, flexible, and collaborative process in which instructors and program administrators work together to reinvent strategies for teaching multimodal composing within their own local contexts. For example, administrators might begin the process of curricular transformation by recruiting a pilot group of teachers to collaboratively develop and enact a new multimodal assignment sequence. Ideally, this pilot group would have the opportunity (during a presemester workshop) to actually attempt to compose the kind of multimodal assignments they intend to assign in their classes, using the same types of technologies to which their students would likely have access. Furthermore, it would be very helpful if the pilot group could meet together occasionally both during and after the semester to reflect about their experiences—working to revise the multimodal curriculum to better address the particular needs of students in their institution. After building some consensus about contextually based, pedagogical strategies among the pilot group, writing program administrators might then attempt a larger curricular transformation in which all teachers in the program would incorporate at least one formal multimodal assignment into their work (with members of the pilot group serving as mentors).

Recognizing that instructors are likely to have differing levels of comfort and expertise in integrating technologies into their pedagogies, it strikes me as important to design a flexible, adaptable assignment sequence that does not depend on the use of any particular technology. So, for example, some teachers in the program might choose to have students transform a printed work into a live spoken presentation while others might push the envelope by exploring digital audio or video. Although the particular kinds of multimodal composing that teachers would engage would then be different, the courses will still be similar in that they are pursuing the common goal of helping students reflect critically about how rhetorical and process concepts do and do not transfer across modalities. In order to sustain a robust multimodal curriculum over time, I also would emphasize the need to provide all teachers in the program with opportunities for ongoing collaborative reflection and participation in curriculum design—the need to develop a programmatic structure that recognizes that *all* teachers of writing have important insights to contribute to the development and enactment of multimodal pedagogies.[1]

Although first-year composition programs can begin to help students consider how rhetorical theories can be applied and adapted across diverse modalities, we must remember of course that the development of rhetorical skill is necessarily a lifelong process that is deeply context dependent (Beaufort). It is therefore unreasonable to expect that a one- or two-course composition sequence can equip students with all the tools they need in order compose persuasive alphabetic, auditory, and visual texts in diverse rhetorical situations. As a result, we must work collaboratively with colleagues to thread the reflective practice of persuasive multimodal composing throughout the entire university curriculum in general education requirements, in interdisciplinary programs, in upper-level disciplinary courses, and in our own writing-centered majors.

Although I do believe that our field's theories of rhetoric and process can productively inform the teaching of multimodal composing throughout the university, I also think it important to acknowledge (as Berthoff, Emig, and Flower and Hayes did) that the study and teaching of multimodal composing must necessarily be an *interdisciplinary* endeavor. For example, scholars of graphic design, visual culture, and architecture have much to teach us about ways that images and built environments can be employed to persuade audiences; cognitive scientists have much to teach us about the similarities and differences in the creative processes of writers, visual artists, and scientific innovators; visual anthropologists and sociologists have much to teach us about the political and ethical implications of employing photography as a research tool; our colleagues in speech and communication departments have much to teach us about the persuasive effects of live oratory; and, of course, musicians, actors, painters, sculptors, performance poets, dancers, animators, filmmakers, and other artists have much to teach us about understanding and practicing composing as a complex, recursive process of making meaning. Rather than seeking simply to impose our own theories of rhetoric and process on the teaching of multimodal composing in other disciplines, we instead need to find ways to collaborate with colleagues in other fields to develop complex, multidisciplinary frameworks for studying and teaching composing across modalities.

As a kind of pilot project to explore the development of interdisciplinary multimodal curricula, we might consider the possibility of collaborating with colleagues across the university in designing first-year learning communities centered on themes such as "Persuasion across Media" or "Creativity across the Arts." By developing a block of team-taught courses or linked (and collaboratively planned) courses that all engage diverse disciplinary perspectives on multimodality, we could foster an inventive learning environment where students and teachers could collaboratively investigate the similarities and differences in composing with visual, alphabetic, and auditory modalities. In order to help students draw connections between courses, instructors in the learning community might ask students to create an online portfolio in which they would synthesize multiple disciplinary frameworks to reflect critically about the creative processes and persuasive strategies they employed in composing diverse multimodal texts. Ideally, this kind of pilot learning community project could begin to lay the groundwork for the development of new general education courses and new interdisciplinary minors and majors that could help students gain a more complex and multifaceted understanding of the reflective practice of persuasive multimodal composing.[2]

Although I believe strongly in the importance of developing interdisciplinary multimodal curricula to serve the needs of contemporary students, I should also note that I think that undergraduate writing and rhetoric majors (housed in English or writing departments) also have a crucial role to play in preparing students to persuasively communicate with words, images, and sounds. As we work to (re) design writing majors to more deeply engage visual and auditory forms of rhetoric, I would suggest that we should seek to thread experience with multiple modalities of composing into *every* class in the major—resisting the tendency to segregate the discussion of multimodality into a few "special" courses on topics such as web authoring or digital and visual rhetoric or multimedia design. For example, a course on rhetorical theory might ask students to explore the classical practice of *enargeia* by composing visual as well as alphabetic arguments; or, a course on "editing and style" might engage students in composing audio podcasts as way to help attune them to rhetorical concerns of concision and voice.

Of course, when we work to integrate multimodal composing throughout a major housed in an English or writing department, we are likely to face questions from faculty, students, administrators, and other stakeholders about whether or not we are exceeding the purview of our discipline. To address this problem, I would suggest we should draw upon our disciplinary heritage (our grounding in theories of rhetoric and composing process) in order to articulate clearly what makes the study of multimodal composing in a writing major different from the study of visual and auditory production in other fields.[3] For example, if I were arguing for the value of a course on "digital video composing" in a writing major, I would assert that my approach to teaching video composing is distinctive because 1) it employs a process-based pedagogy that is specifically informed by the field of composition studies; 2) it applies *rhetorical theory* to the analysis and production of video texts; and 3) it places a special emphasis on exploring the intersections between alphabetic writing and video production. In other words, a course on digital video composing in a writing major will be different from one in film or mass communication because it approaches video from the unique disciplinary lens of composition studies—a field that has been critically engaging the intersections of moving images and writing at least since the 1960s.

In order to develop and sustain robust multimodal writing majors, we must also begin to rethink the ways we are educating the next generation of faculty in our graduate programs. As we work to (re)design MA and PhD curricula to prepare graduate students to effectively teach persuasive multimodal composing, we must remember that rhetoric is first and foremost a *productive* art. It is not enough for graduate students to learn how to analyze the persuasive effects of images and sounds; they also must gain extensive experience with composing persuasive multimodal texts for diverse audiences and purposes. Rather than positioning multimodal composing as a supplemental topic only relevant to graduate students who profess a specialty in "computers-and-writing," we might instead seek to demonstrate ways that *all* scholars of composition and rhetoric can benefit by incorporating visual and audio elements into their research. For example, qualitative literacy studies researchers might create video documentaries based on interviews or historians of rhetoric might develop online, multimodal archives. In order to prepare all graduate students to produce multimodal scholarship, our masters and doctoral curricula will likely need to feature at least one core course (preferably more) in which students gain hands-on experience composing multimodal arguments (web texts, videos, live performances) using a range of digital technologies. Furthermore, it is important that we encourage and make it possible for graduate students to take courses in visual and audio production offered in other allied arts departments. Finally, I would recom-

mend that graduate faculty consider redesigning the requirements
for candidacy exams and dissertations to make space for students
to persuasively construct knowledge through visual and auditory
modalities of communication.

Although numerous rhetoric and composition graduate programs
have already begun rethinking curricula and requirements in the
ways I outline here, it is still the case that many faculty and graduate students in our field continue to gravitate to print-based work
as the default standard—continue to be wary that any time they
spend on multimodal composing will not be valued by the wider
academy. In many ways, this is not surprising given the fact that
the print-based article and monograph continue to be positioned
as the most valued forms of research publication in many (though
not all) of the institutions in which graduates of our programs are
placed. Thus, if we truly wish to transform our graduate curricula
to make space for multimodal composing, it is imperative that we
also work to transform the print-based standards of evaluation that
continue to govern tenure and promotion decisions in many of our
institutions—that we work to convince our colleagues throughout
the university to embrace a capacious vision of scholarship that
recognizes and values the unique affordances of visual and auditory
forms of communication (C. Ball; Lee and Selfe).

GOAL 3: DEVELOP CRITICAL LITERACIES BY EMPLOYING A RANGE OF MULTIMODAL STRATEGIES FOR RESEEING, REHEARING, AND ULTIMATELY TRANSFORMING THE WORLD

When we relisten to the voices of Smitherman, Freire, Shor, and
others, we can be reminded that we have an ethical responsibility
to resist the hegemony of print forms of knowledge in the academy—an ethical responsibility to value and support all the diverse
auditory, visual, and alphabetic ways of knowing that students bring
to our classes. Although it is important to encourage students to
recognize the power of alphabetic forms of communication, we also
must help them come to understand that the written word (like all
modalities) is limited in what it can discover and convey about the

world. In addition to engaging students in conducting research by reading and writing alphabetic texts, then we also need to provide opportunities for them to collaboratively construct knowledge by conducting oral interviews, by engaging in spoken dialogue, by taking photographs, by participating in performance activities (to name but a few methods). By enabling students to employ multiple forms of composing to critically rehear and resee the world, we might increase the likelihood that they will come to recognize and attempt to transform the unjust material hierarchies of race, class, gender, sexuality, and disability that prevent the realization of transformative democracy in our nation and our world.

When we remember our field's historic and ongoing commitment to advocating for democracy and social justice, we can come to realize that making a multimodal turn should not simply be a matter of teaching students to compose "effective" and "appropriate" digital products that serve the interests of dominant power structures. Rather, a truly critical multimodal pedagogy must entail a process of teaching students to analyze and *contest* the ideological implications of corporate media. In our classes at all levels (from first-year composition to doctoral seminars), we need to provide students with opportunities to both critically interrogate and *remake* the kinds of persuasive digital texts that are increasingly influential in civic life. For example, not only should students analyze how social networking sites influence the rhetorical construction of identity, but they should also have the chance to employ social networking platforms in order compose and distribute persuasive activist texts to public audiences. And not only should students learn to critique the ideological implications of the ways mainstream media outlets construct reality, but they should also have the opportunity to employ online video composing to craft an alternate vision of the news of the day.

Although it is important for compositionists to consider how emerging social media platforms offer new possibilities for civic participation, we also must be mindful that ableist, classist, racist, and sexist power structures continue to negatively influence people's abilities to access and transform digital technologies (Banks; Dolmage; Ellis and Kent; Grabill; C. Selfe and Hawisher; Slatin).

If we are truly to teach students to employ multimodal composing as a vehicle for social change, then we will need to join with broader social movements in challenging the persistent inequalities in access to both education and technology that prevent many people from having their voices heard in the new media landscape. In addition to working to advocate for more equitable access, we also should seek to resist the common tendency to focus our pedagogical attention too narrowly on keeping up with the latest technological trends (Shipka, "A Multimodal"). Indeed, we must remember that if we place too much emphasis on elucidating the transformative potential of new technologies, we run the risk of ignoring or effacing the ways in which *all* people have important insights to contribute about auditory and visual composing, whether or not they use computer-based tools.

Ultimately, if we seek to value the diverse embodied knowledges of *all* students and teachers in the field of composition, we must embrace a capacious vision of multimodal pedagogy that includes both digital and nondigital forms of communication: live oratory and digital audio documentary; quilting and video gaming; paper-based scrapbooking and digital storytelling; protest chanting and activist video making.[4] After all, we must remember that compositionists have been pursuing critical multimodal pedagogies at least since the late 1960s—long before the first PCs came on the scene. Rather than focusing solely on how multimodal pedagogies can be designed in response to emerging technologies, then, we might instead work to reemphasize how the contemporary multimodal turn can best be conceptualized as a continuation of our field's longstanding commitments to rhetoric, to process, and to social justice.

In outlining the above three pedagogical goals, I have deliberately created a quite utopian vision of the multimodal future of our field. Yet, when I look back at composition history, I can't help but be reminded that simply calling for change—simply crafting a vision—is not enough. After all, as this book has shown, compositionists have been calling for a multimodal transformation of our field for at least forty years; and, yet, despite these calls, the study and teaching of composition has remained (in many ways) too narrowly focused on alphabetic ways of knowing. Although this history of unrealized multimodal visions ultimately makes me somewhat skeptical and cautious about the possibilities for transforming our field, I can't help but retain my sincere belief in the power of what Cynthia Selfe calls "small potent gestures." We may not be able to realize multi-modal utopia, but we can work together in small ways to begin to change our pedagogies, our universities, and our social and political structures. And, I like to think of this book as my own small potent gesture toward this effort—my own modest attempt to begin remaking our future by reinventing our past. I know all too well that there is much that this book does not accomplish, much that it does not address, much that it fails to even consider . . . but if I can inspire one more composition teacher to make a small potent gesture then I will be happy.

Prologue

1. Although I glibly begin this book with the assertion that "I once knew what it meant to be a compositionist," I must note that I recognize that the definition of "what it means to be a compositionist" is deeply contextual and necessarily complex. In some sense, my understanding of "what it means to be a compositionist" shifts daily depending on the embodied locations I inhabit and the professional practices in which I engage. Nevertheless, I would contend that before I made the multimodal turn, I had a more stable sense of professional identity as a compositionist—a clearer ability to explain to others what qualified me to teach the courses that I did.

2. While many people still understand the term "writing" to refer only to the production of alphabetic text, some composition scholars have begun to broaden the definition of "writing" to include auditory and visual communication as well (Lunsford; WIDE). As a result, I choose to use the more specific term, *alphabetic writing*, when I want to very clearly restrict my argument to the production of written, alphabetic words—whether in print or on-screen. At times, I also choose to employ the more generic term "writing," when I wish to emphasize the production of alphabetic text, but also leave open the possibility that my argument might apply to other forms of meaning making as well. In contrast, I consistently employ the term "composing" when I want to make clear that I am referring broadly to *all* forms of symbolic making meaning (visual, auditory, alphabetic, gestural, spatial). Because the term "composing" is shared by scholars of writing, visual, and performing arts, I believe it usefully highlights the ways that the study of multimodal communication must necessarily be an interdisciplinary endeavor.

Introduction: Reseeing Composition History

1. For the record, I should note that I am not personally a big fan of the Bee Gees, though I do imagine that I could have a lot of fun mashing

up their work with samples from contemporary hip hop and indie rock. For those who may be curious about how my taste in music has informed this project, I can report that my writing of this book has often been propelled and nurtured by a digital mix of songs from the Arcade Fire, Ani DiFranco, Vampire Weekend, Matt & Kim, Pavement, Pansy Division, Velvet Underground, and the Pixies.

2. While Berlin's taxonomy of expressivist, cognitive, and social-epistemic approaches continues to be influential in the field, it also has increasingly been critiqued by composition historians for oversimplifying the ideological and epistemological positions of the pedagogical scholarship it seeks to categorize (Ede; Gold; Gradin; Hawk; Roskelly and Ronald).

1. Creative Translations: Reimagining the Process Movement (1971–84)

1. Flash is a program that enables composers to create digital animations that combine images, sound, and text. Because it is intended for media professionals, Flash can have a bit of a steep learning curve. Thus, in my multimodal teaching, I have tended not to employ Flash, choosing instead to teach students to use free and relatively simple video and audio editors such as iMovie, Movie Maker, and Audacity.

2. For an excellent collection of "post-process" critiques of the writing process movement, see Kent. In many ways, I agree with Kent (and other post-process theorists) that attempts to develop generalizable theories of the writing process risk ignoring how the act of writing is both profoundly social and radically situated. Yet, even though I recognize the limitations of generalizable theories, I suggest that it remains pedagogically useful to continue to attempt to develop flexible heuristics for understanding composing that can be applied across multiple situations and modalities.

3. Although compositionists have largely avoided engaging interdisciplinary scholarship on creative cognition in the last twenty years, numerous contemporary composition scholars have written insightful theoretical explorations of the interrelation between writing and other arts (Delagrange; Fishman et al.; Janangelo; Rice; Sirc; Ulmer). Significantly, however, these scholars have not discussed ways that their investigations of composing across modalities can be considered extensions of the foundational work of the process movement.

4. In cognitive terms, a mental image is a nonverbal sensory perception "represented and processed in the absence of external perceptual stimulus" (J. Anderson 106). Although mental images are often visual, it is also possible to have auditory, tactile, gustatory, or olfactory images as well (Kosslyn; Paivio).

5. Flower and Hayes's metaphor of writing as translation has been strongly critiqued by scholars such as Patricia Bizzell and James Berlin for failing to recognize the ways our thinking is socially constructed through the means of language. I agree that the metaphor of translation risks suggesting incorrectly that writing is merely a process of transcribing ideas that exist prior to the social mediation of language. Nevertheless, I argue that the metaphor of translation is productive because it reminds us that we don't just think in words alone—that multiple symbol systems (imagistic, linguistic) interact within the mind.

6. For an illuminating analysis of how Berthoff draws on Langer and Cassirer in theorizing the role of imagery in composition, see J. Murray (*Non-Discursive* 32–35, 48–50). In his work, Murray focuses especially on showing ways in which the philosophical tradition that informed Berthoff can help compositionists analyze and teach "non-discursive rhetoric." In this chapter, I focus on elucidating how Berthoff theorized and taught alphabetic writing as a social composing process that shares affinities with other artistic forms of composing (visual, tactile, gestural, spatial).

7. For an insightful discussion of multimodal approaches to writing across the curriculum, see Bridwell-Bowles, Powell, and Choplin.

8. I offer more detailed discussions of audio composing in chapter 2, multimedia collage in chapter 3, and video composing in chapter 4. For a useful introduction to pedagogical and technological approaches for integrating video and audio composing into the writing classroom, see Cynthia Selfe's *Multimodal Composition: Resources for Teachers.*

2. Composing Voices: Writing Pedagogy as Auditory Art (1965–87)

1. I quote here from a text that Elbow published in 1994; however, I would argue that this emphasis on voice as "embodied sound" also played a role in Elbow's earlier theorizing of the concept in the 1970s and 1980s.

2. These are just a few of the many ways that performance activities can be integrated into the writing class. In recent years, numerous scholars have published insightful accounts of the uses of performance in composition pedagogy (Claycomb; Fishman et al.; Skinner-Linnenberg). Virginia Skinner-Linnenberg's work is particularly notable because she offers a detailed discussion of how teachers might build upon Moffett's dramatic work in order to reclaim the importance of the rhetorical canon of delivery in the writing classroom (90–96).

3. In *Talkin and Testifyin*, Smitherman defines "Black English" as a dialect, and I follow that usage here; however, in recent years, Smitherman and other scholars have increasingly made the case that African American English can be termed a distinct *language*. Although academic linguists

recognize the validity of all dialects (and reject the notion that any one form of a language can be seen as standard), Smitherman notes in a recent book that the term "dialect" continues to carry negative connotations in the popular imagination; thus, it may be more rhetorically and politically effective to employ the term "African American *Language*" to articulate the uniqueness, value, and power of African American ways of speaking (Smitherman *Word* 15–18). Furthermore, Smitherman importantly suggests that the use of the term "Black English dialect" problematically risks effacing how African American speech has been deeply influenced by both African and English linguistic traditions. Although I have chosen for historical reasons to employ the term "dialect" in this book, I should note that I fully support the right of *all* people to define their own ways of speaking and writing using whatever terms they see fit.

4. Among historians of composition, Smitherman has been especially remembered for her crucial role in advocating and codrafting the 1974 CCCC resolution "Students' Right to Their Own Language"—a resolution that radically and importantly called for composition teachers to resist racist and classist notions of "Standard English" by valuing and supporting all of the diverse dialects that students speak and write (Gilyard, "African American"; Parks; Smitherman, "CCCC"; Wible).

5. Although it can be difficult to draw upon tonal semantics in alphabetic text, it is not impossible. For a fascinating discussion of how contemporary African American rhetors employ tonal semantics when writing in online spaces, see Banks (80).

6. Within the past five years, numerous compositionists have published important scholarship outlining approaches for integrating digital audio production into the writing classroom; in addition to looking to the past for inspiration, I also recommend that teachers interested in digital audio composing consult this emerging body of work (Braun, McCorkle, and Wolf; Comstock and Hocks; Dangler, McCorkle, and Barrow; Halbritter; McKee; Reid, "Tuning"; Shipka, "Sound"; R. Selfe and Selfe; Shankar; Zdenek).

3. The First Time Print Died: Revisiting Composition's Multimedia Turn (1967–74)

1. For a useful, critical history of the "rise and fall" of the modes of discourse approach, see Connors.

2. I would like to note that I think that Burnett, Thomason, and Wiener should all be commended for their sincere and innovative attempts to try to make composition more engaging for students; furthermore, I recognize that their choice to emphasize the importance of "error correction" may very well have been a conscious rhetorical strategy designed to appeal to

their intended audience of traditional composition instructors. Although I personally align myself with Smitherman in the debate over "error" in the field, I also recognize that Burnett, Thomason, and Wiener were merely appealing to commonplace assumptions about "correctness" that were widely held by composition instructors at the time. My goal here is simply to point out that multimedia pedagogies (both then and now) are sometimes not as radical or innovative as they might at first appear—that it is very possible to employ new media in ways that work to reinforce traditional (and perhaps problematic) pedagogical practices.

3. In a 1971 review of several "multi-media textbooks" in *CCC,* Lewis Sego positions *Montage* as the most radically innovative textbook under consideration, noting that the authors "have struck out at the medium of print with such boldness that the conventions of bookmaking have turned and fled" (55). Although Sego suggests that more traditional instructors and students will find it unduly challenging to engage *Montage,* he also argues that "because of its wealth of innovations many new teachers will be dissatisfied with anything less. *Montage* may even appeal to certain experienced teachers who want out of the rut at any cost" (55).

4. Kytle's *Comp Box* was published by Aspen Communications, who also published *Aspen: The Multimedia Magazine in a Box.* Rejecting the bound format of the conventional periodical, Aspen magazine took the form of a box that contained printed materials in various sizes, phonograph recordings, and (in one case) a super 8 film. Unfortunately, in 1971, *Aspen* magazine ceased to be published after the postal service refused to consider it a "periodical" for the purposes of mailing and thus charged the publisher an exorbitant rate for postage (King 68). Although boxed copies of *Aspen* magazine are quite rare, the contents of the magazine boxes have recently been digitized and made available on the web (Stafford). To my knowledge, the *Comp Box* was Aspen Communications' first attempt to adapt the magazine box concept to educational textbook publishing. The *Comp Box* was advertised in *College Composition and Communication* in 1971, 1972, and 1973 (Aspen; Xerox).

5. I should note that I see a good deal of value in both multimodal PSAs and autobiographical digital stories as assignments in composition classes. In fact, I have employed both kinds of assignments in my work as a multimodal writing teacher (with varying degrees of success). I am merely pointing out, based on my experience, that these kinds of assignments are not as inherently transformative as digital advocates sometimes make them out to be—that we must carefully reflect about how we might inadvertently use new media tools to reinforce problematic assumptions about composing.

6. In addition to looking back to the early 1970s for theories of the role of multimodal juxtaposition in invention, we can also turn to the work of more contemporary scholars (Delagrange; Hawk; Reid, *Two*; Rice; Sirc; Ulmer).

7. In *Race, Rhetoric, and Technology*, Adam Banks powerfully demonstrates that for access to computers to "have any effect on people's lives or on their participation in the society, people must also have the knowledge and skills necessary to use these tools effectively (*functional access*). They must be connected enough with those technologies that they use them (*experiential access*). They must also understand the benefits and problems of those technologies well enough to be able to critique them when necessary and use them when necessary (*critical access*)" (Banks 138). And, finally, Banks importantly argues that even critique is not enough. Ultimately, real "transformative access" requires that all people gain the power to *redesign* existing technologies in order "to be able to tell their own stories in their own terms and able to meet the real material, social, cultural, and political needs in their lives and in their communities" (Banks 138). I wholeheartedly agree with Banks's argument here, and I would like to note that this kind of activism for "transformative access" is crucial if we are ever to develop and enact digital multimodal pedagogies that truly contribute to social change.

4. Zooming Out: Notes toward a History of "Cameras-and-Writing" (1971–84)

1. Of course, as I argued in chapter 3, it is important for us to take a critical view of this kind narrative of technological crisis. After all, with the value of hindsight, we can recognize that some members of the multimedia-loving "Woodstock generation" have since grown up to become the very same senior faculty who now bemoan that today's young people are not as interested in books as they used to be.

2. In her history of the visual in composition, Diana George offers a useful (if brief) analysis of Costanzo's 1986 *CCC* article "Film as Composition"; however, she doesn't discuss his 1984 textbook, *Double Exposure*. In my view, Costanzo's *Double Exposure* provides a much more detailed and theoretically nuanced vision for integrating film and writing instruction than his relatively short *CCC* article was able to outline.

3. Costanzo's discussion of invention is strongly influenced by Berthoff's essay "Learning the Uses of Chaos" (*Making* 68–72).

4. Although I think that false consciousness can be a potentially useful heuristic for considering the ideological functions of media texts, I ultimately agree with Ellen Cushman's critique that the theories of false consciousness run the risk of effacing the numerous powerful ways that

many oppressed people already critically read and attempt to transform hegemonic social structures (Cushman 4–9).

5. Of course, it is important to note that many of the videos on YouTube receive few if any views; merely uploading a rhetorically sophisticated video is usually not enough for students to garner an audience. In order to increase viewership for their activist work, students need to learn how to use tags and descriptions to increase the "findability" of their videos on YouTube as well as how to employ social networks (such as Facebook) in order to publicize and circulate their video work. Furthermore, I must point out that YouTube remains a space where sexism, homophobia, racism, ableism, and classism abound; although I think it can be possible to harness YouTube as a tool for promoting social change, I don't mean to suggest that the technology of online video sharing is inherently progressive or transformative.

6. Recently, there has been a move to reconceptualize the field of "computers-and-writing" more broadly as "digital writing" (WIDE). Although this redefinition productively emphasizes the diverse digital technologies that contemporary students use to compose, it still runs the risk of effacing the history of how past compositionists engaged *analog* composing technologies such as the super 8 camera.

7. For a contemporary textbook that offers a useful approach for integrating photography and writing instruction, see *Picturing Texts* (Faigley et al.).

8. In addition to looking to Costanzo for a vision of integrating video production and writing instruction, we might also turn to more recent computers-and-writing scholarship that has demonstrated productive ways that composition teachers might integrate digital video composing into their pedagogies (D. Anderson; Beard; Comstock and Hocks; Delagrange; Lovett et al.; Ross; C. Selfe, *Multimodal*).

9. Although I focus here mostly on the rhetorical aspects of documentary, I should note that it is crucial that teachers and students spend time discussing the politics and ethics of representation in documentary composing as well. In my own classes, I have frequently used Bill Nichols's *Introduction to Documentary* and the Center for Social Media's "Honest Truths: Documentary Filmmakers on the Ethical Challenges in Their Work" as texts to help students develop a theoretical framework for analyzing the political and ethical choices that documentarians make.

10. This example is inspired by a very a powerful audio remix that Amir Hassan composed in my doctoral seminar, "New Media and Composition Studies."

11. I recognize that some teachers may be concerned that these suggested remix activities appear to encourage students to violate copyright law.

I would argue, however, that this kind of remix video composing is protected by the doctrine of *fair use*, and I would employ the Center for Social Media's "Code of Best Practices for Fair Use in Online Video" to back up my claim. But, of course, I should note that I am not a legal scholar, and that the definition of what constitutes fair use is both slippery and contested. Whenever I include remix composing in my courses, I always ask students to watch and read a range of critical texts about intellectual property concerns (Center, "Code"; Faden; "Get Creative"; Lessig, "On Laws"), and I also ask them to write reflectively about the ethical choices they are making in sampling copyrighted works. In this way, I hope to prepare students to become reflective, activist composers who can *make* informed ethical choices about intellectual property and *defend* those choices to others (DeVoss and Webb; Digirhet; Johnson-Eilola and Selber; Logie; Ridolfo and DeVoss; Rife).

Epilogue

1. For a robust and helpful discussion of the possibilities and challenges of sustaining digital writing programs, see DeVoss, McKee, and Selfe.

2. At the University of Illinois, faculty in English and visual design have successfully collaborated to develop a powerful interdisciplinary course "Writing with Video." For an insightful discussion of this innovative collaborative venture, see Lovett et al.

3. In addition to being informed by the discipline of composition studies, many writing majors also are grounded in the related fields of professional writing and technical communication—both of which have substantial traditions of engaging the rhetorical aspects of visual and multimedia design.

4. In calling for a multimodal pedagogy that embraces both digital and nondigital forms of composing, I am indebted to the work of Jody Shipka and Anne Wysocki.

WORKS CITED

Anderson, Daniel. "The Low Bridge to High Benefits: Entry Level Multimedia, Literacies, and Motivation." *Computers and Composition* 25.1 (2008): 40–60.

Anderson, John R. *Cognitive Psychology and Its Implications.* New York: Worth, 2000.

Angell, C. F. "Response to Richard Williamson, 'The Case for Filmmaking as English Composition.'" *College Composition and Communication* 22.3 (1971): 256–59.

Arnheim, Rudolf. *Visual Thinking.* Berkeley: U of California P, 1969.

Aspen Communications, Inc. Advertisement. *College Composition and Communication* 22.5 (1971): N. pag.

———. Advertisement. *College Composition and Communication* 23.1 (1972): 114–15.

Baca, Damian. *Mestiz@Scripts, Digital Migrations, and the Territories of Writing.* New York: Palgrave MacMillan, 2008.

Ball, Arnetha F., and Ted Lardner. *African American Literacies Unleashed: Vernacular English and the Composition Classroom.* Carbondale: Southern Illinois UP, 2005.

Ball, Cheryl E. "Show Not Tell: The Value of New Media Scholarship." *Computers and Composition* 21.4 (2004): 403–25.

Ball, Cheryl, and Byron Hawk, eds. "Special Issue: Sound in/as Compositional Space: A Next Step in Multiliteracies." *Computers and Composition* 23.3 (2006).

Banks, Adam J. *Race, Rhetoric, and Technology: Searching for Higher Ground.* Mahwah, NJ: Earlbaum, 2006.

Baron, Dennis. *A Better Pencil: Readers, Writers, and the Digital Revolution.* New York: Oxford UP, 2009.

Beard, Jeannie Parker. "Documenting Arguments, Proposing Change: Reflections on Student-Produced Proposal Documentaries." *Computers and Composition Online* Spring 2010. Aug. 29, 2011. <http://www.bgsu.edu/cconline/Parker_Beard_New/>.

Beaufort, Anne. *College Writing and Beyond: A New Framework for University Writing Instruction*. Logan: Utah State UP, 2007.

Berlin, James. "Rhetoric and Ideology in the Writing Class." *College English* 50.5 (1998): 477–94.

———. *Rhetoric and Reality: Writing Instruction in American Colleges, 1980–1985*. Carbondale: Southern Illinois UP, 1987.

Berthoff, Ann E. *Forming, Thinking, Writing: The Composing Imagination*. Montclair, NJ: Boynton/Cook, 1982.

———. *The Making of Meaning: Metaphors, Models, and Maxims for Writing Teachers*. Montclair, NJ: Boynton/Cook, 1981.

———. *Reclaiming the Imagination: Philosophical Perspectives for Teachers of Writing*. Upper Montclair, NJ: Boynton/Cook, 1984.

Bizzell, Patricia. "Cognition, Convention, and Certainty: What We Need to Know about Writing." *Pre/Text* 3 (1982): 213–44.

Bolter, Jay David, and Richard Grusin. *Remediation: Understanding New Media*. Cambridge, MA: MIT P, 1999.

Braun, Catherine C., Ben McCorkle, and Amie C. Wolf. "Remixing Basic Writing: Digital Media Production and the Basic Writing Curriculum." *Computers and Composition Online* Spring 2007. Aug. 29, 2011. <http://www.bgsu.edu/cconline/braun/index.htm>.

Briand, Paul. "Turned On: Multi-Media and Advanced Composition." *College Composition and Communication* 21.3 (1970): 267–69.

Bridwell-Bowles, Lillian, Karen E. Powell, and Tiffany Walter Choplin. "Not Just Words Anymore: Multimodal Communication across the Curriculum." *Across the Disciplines* 6 (2009). Aug. 29, 2011. <http://wac.colostate.edu/atd/technologies/bridwellbowlesetal.cfm>.

Burke, Kenneth. *Language as Symbolic Action: Essays on Life, Literature, and Method*. Berkeley: U of California P, 1966.

Burnett, Esther, and Sandra Thomason. "The Cassette-Slide Show in Required Composition." *College Composition and Communication* 25.5 (1974): 426–30.

Campbell, Kermit E. *Gettin' Our Groove On: Rhetoric, Language, and Literacy for the Hip Hop Generation*. Detroit: Wayne State UP, 2005.

Center for Social Media. "Code of Best Practices for Fair Use in Online Video." June 2008. Aug. 29, 2011. <http://www.centerforsocialmedia.org/sites/default/files/online_best_practices_in_fair_use.pdf>.

———. "Honest Truths: Documentary Filmmakers on the Ethical Challenges in Their Work." Sept. 2009. Aug. 29, 2011. <http://www.centerforsocialmedia.org/sites/default/files/Honest_Truths_Documentary_Filmmakers_on_Ethical_Challenges_in_Their_Work.pdf>.

Childers, Pamela B., Eric H. Hobson, and Joan A. Mullin. *ARTiculating: Teaching Writing in a Visual World.* Portsmouth, NH: Heinemann, 1998.

Clare, Warren L., and Kenneth J. Ericksen. *Multimmediate: Multi Media and the Art of Writing.* New York: Random, 1972.

Claycomb, Ryan. "Performing/Teaching/Writing: Performance Studies in the Composition Classroom." *Enculturation* 6.1 (2008). Aug. 29, 2011. <http://enculturation.gmu.edu/6.1/claycomb>.

Comprone, Joseph. "Response to Richard Williamson ('The Case for Film-making as Composition') and to C. F. Angell." *College Composition and Communication* 23.1 (1972): 55–58.

Comstock, Michelle, and Mary E. Hocks. "Voice in the Cultural Sound-scape: Sonic Literacy in Composition Studies." *Computers and Composition Online* Spring 2006). Aug. 29, 2011. <http://www.bgsu.edu/cconline/comstock_hocks/>.

Connors, Robert J. "The Rise and Fall of the Modes of Discourse." *College Composition and Communication* 32.4 (1981): 444–55.

Connors, Robert J., Lisa S. Ede, and Andrea A. Lunsford. "The Revival of Rhetoric in America." *Essays on Classical Rhetoric and Modern Discourse.* Ed. Robert J. Connors, Lisa S. Ede, and Andrea A. Lunsford. Carbondale: Southern Illinois UP, 1984. 1–15.

Corbett, Edward P. J. "A New Look at Old Rhetoric." *Rhetoric: Theories for Application.* Ed. Robert M. Gorell. Champaign, IL: NCTE, 1967. 16–22.

———. "Rhetoric in Search of a Past, Present, and Future." *The Prospect of Rhetoric.* Ed. Lloyd F. Bitzer. Englewood Cliffs, NJ: Prentice-Hall, 1971. 167–78.

———. "The Rhetoric of the Open Hand and the Rhetoric of the Closed Fist." *College Composition and Communication* 20 (1969): 288–96.

———. "Rhetoric, the Enabling Discipline." *Ohio English Bulletin* 13 (1972): 2–10.

———. *Selected Essays of Edward P. J. Corbett.* Dallas: Southern Methodist UP, 1989.

———. "What Is Being Revived?" *College Composition and Communication* 18 (1967): 166–72.

Costanzo, William. *Double Exposure: Composing through Writing and Film.* Upper Montclair, NJ: Boynton/Cook, 1984.

———. "Film as Composition." *College Composition and Communication* 37.1 (1986): 79–86.

Cowley, Malcolm, ed. *Writers at Work: The Paris Interviews.* New York: Viking, 1958.

Crowley, Sharon. *Composition in the University: Historical and Polemical Essays.* Pittsburgh: U of Pittsburgh P, 1998.

Cushman, Ellen. *The Struggle and the Tools: Oral and Literate Strategies in an Inner City Community.* Albany: State U of New York P, 1998.

Dangler, Doug, Ben McCorkle, and Time Barrow. "Expanding Composition Audiences with Podcasting." *Computers and Composition Online* Spring 2007. Aug. 29, 2011. <http://www.bgsu.edu/cconline/podcasting/>.

Deemer, Charles. "English Composition as a Happening." *College English* 29 (1967): 121–26.

Delagrange, Susan. "*Wunderkammer,* Cornell, and the Visual Canon of Arrangement." *Kairos: A Journal of Rhetoric, Technology, and Pedagogy* 13.2 (2009). Aug. 29, 2011. <http://kairos.technorhetoric.net/13.2/topoi/delagrange/index.html>.

DeVoss, Dànielle Nicole, Ellen Cushman, and Jeffery Grabill. "Infrastructure and Composing: The When of New-Media Writing." *College Composition and Communication* 57.1 (2005): 14–44.

DeVoss, Dànielle Nicole, Heidi McKee, and Richard Selfe, eds. *Technological Ecologies and Sustainability.* Computers and Composition Digital Press, 2009. Aug. 29, 2011. <http://ccdigitalpress.org/tes/>.

DeVoss, Dànielle Nicole, and James E. Porter. "Why Napster Matters to Writing: Filesharing as a New Ethic of Digital Delivery." *Computers and Composition* 23.2 (2006): 178–210.

DeVoss, Dànielle Nicole, and Suzanne Webb. "Media Convergence: Grand Theft Audio: Negotiating Copyright as Composers." *Computers and Composition* 25.1 (2008): 79–103.

Digirhet. "Old + Old + Old = New: A Copyright Manifesto for a Digital World." *Kairos: A Journal of Rhetoric, Technology, and Pedagogy* 12.3 (2008). Aug. 29, 2011. <http://kairos.technorhetoric.net/12.3/topoi/digirhet/index.html>.

Diogenes, Marvin, and Andrea A. Lunsford. "Toward Delivering New Definitions of Writing." *Delivering College Composition: The Fifth Canon.* Ed. Kathleen Blake Yancey. Portsmouth, NH: Boynton/Cook, 2006. 141–54.

Dolmage, Jay. "Disability, Usability, and Universal Design." *Rhetorically Re-Thinking Usability.* Ed. Shelley Rodrigo and Susan Miller. Cresskill, NJ: Hampton, 2008.

Dubisar, Abby, and Jason Palmeri. "Palin/Pathos/Peter Griffin: Political Video Remix and Composition Pedagogy." *Computers and Composition* 27.2 (2010): 77–93.

Dunn, Patricia A. *Talking, Sketching, Moving: Multiple Literacies for Composition.* Portsmouth, NH: Heinemann, 2001.

Dunstan, Maryjane, and Patricia Wallace Garlan. *Worlds in the Making: Probes for Students of the Future.* Englewood Cliffs, NJ: Prentice-Hall, 1970.

Ede, Lisa. *Situating Composition: Composition Studies and the Politics of Location.* Carbondale: Southern Illinois UP, 2004.

Elbow, Peter. "What Do We Mean When We Talk about Voice in Texts?" *Voices on Voice.* Ed. Kathleen Blake Yancey. Urbana, IL: NCTE, 1994. 1–35.

———. *Writing with Power: Techniques for Mastering the Writing Process.* Oxford: Oxford UP, 1981.

———. *Writing without Teachers.* New York: Oxford UP, 1973.

Eldred, Janet M. "Pedagogy in the Computer-Networked Classroom." *Computers and Composition* 8.2 (1991): 47–61.

Ellertson, Anthony. "Some Notes on Simulacra Machines, Flash in First-Year Composition, and Tactics in Spaces of Interruption." *Kairos: A Journal of Rhetoric, Technology, and Pedagogy* 8.2 (2003). Aug. 29, 2011. <http://kairos.technorhetoric.net/8.2/index.html>.

Ellis, Katie, and Mike Kent. *Disability and New Media.* London: Routledge, 2010.

Emig, Janet. *The Composing Process of Twelfth Graders.* NCTE Research Report No. 13. Urbana, IL: NCTE, 1971.

Faden, Eric. "A Fair(y) Use Tale." *YouTube.* Aug. 1, 2010. Aug. 29, 2011. <http://www.youtube.com/watch?v=CJn_jC4FNDo>.

Faigley, Lester. "Competing Theories of Process: A Critique and a Proposal." *College English* 48.6 (1986): 527–42.

Faigley, Lester, et al. *Picturing Texts.* New York: Norton, 2004.

Finke, Ronald A., Thomas B. Ward, and Steven M. Smith. *Creative Cognition: Theory, Research, Applications.* Cambridge, MA: MIT P, 1992.

Fishman, Jenn, et al. "Performing Writing, Performing Literacy." *College Composition and Communication* 57.2 (2005): 224–52.

Fleckenstein, Kristie S. *Embodied Literacies: Imageword and a Poetics of Teaching.* Carbondale: Southern Illinois UP, 2003.

Flower, Linda, and John R. Hayes. "The Cognition of Discovery: Defining a Rhetorical Problem." *College Composition and Communication* 31.1 (1980): 21–32.

———. "A Cognitive Process Theory of Writing." *College Composition and Communication* 32.4 (1981): 365–87.

———. "Images, Plans, and Prose: The Representation of Meaning in Writing." *Written Communication* 1.1 (1984): 120–60.

Foster, Helen. *Networked Process: Dissolving Boundaries of Process and Post-Process.* West Lafayette, IN: Parlor, 2007.

Frank, Joseph. *You.* New York: Harcourt, Brace, and Jonavich, 1972.

Freire, Paulo. *Pedagogy of the Oppressed.* London: Continuum, 1970.

Gardner, Howard. E *Art, Mind, and Brain: A Cognitive Approach to Creativity.* New York: Basic, 1982.

———. *Frames of Mind: The Theory of Multiple Intelligences.* New York: Basic, 1983.

Geisler, Cheryl, and Shaun Slattery. "Capturing the Activity of Digital Writing: Using, Analyzing, and Supplementing Video Screen Capture." *Digital Writing Research: Technologies, Methodologies, and Ethical Issues.* Ed. Heidi A. McKee and Danielle Nicole DeVoss. Cresskill, NJ: Hampton, 2007. 185–200.

George, Diana. "From Analysis to Design: Visual Communication in the Teaching of Writing." *College Composition and Communication* 54.1 (2002): 11–39.

Gerard, Lisa. "The Evolution of the Computers and Writing Conference, the Second Decade." *Computers and Composition* 23.2 (2006): 211–27.

"Get Creative." *Creativecommons.org.* Aug. 1, 2010. Aug. 29, 2011. <http://creativecommons.org/videos/get-creative>.

Getzels, Jacob W., and Mihaly Csikszentmihalyi. *The Creative Vision: A Longitudinal Study of Problem Finding in Art.* New York: John Wiley and Sons, 1976.

Gilyard, Keith. "African American Contributions to Composition Studies." *College Composition and Communication* 50.4 (1999): 626–44.

———. *Let's Flip the Script: An African-American Discourse on Language, Literature, and Learning.* Detroit: Wayne State UP, 1996.

Gitelman, Lisa. *Always Already New: Media, History, and the Data of Culture.* Cambridge, MA: MIT P, 2006.

Gitelman, Lisa, and Geoffrey B. Pingree. "Introduction: What's New about New Media?" *New Media, 1740–1915.* Ed. Lisa Gitelman and Geoffrey B. Pingree. Cambridge, MA: MIT P, 2003. xi–xxii.

Glenn, Cheryl. *Unspoken: A Rhetoric of Silence.* Carbondale: Southern Illinois UP, 2004.

Gold, David. *Rhetoric at the Margins: Revising the History of Writing Instruction in American Colleges, 1873–1947.* Carbondale: Southern Illinois UP, 2008.

Grabill, Jeffrey T. "On Divides and Interfaces: Access, Class, and Computers." *Computers and Composition* 20.4 (2003): 455–72.

Gradin, Sherrie L. *Romancing Rhetorics: Social Expressivist Perspectives on the Teaching of Writing.* Portsmouth, NH: Boynton/Cook, 1995.

Haas, Angela M. "Wampum as Hypertext: An American Indian Intellectual Tradition of Multimedia Theory and Practice." *Studies in American Indian Literatures* 19.4 (2007): 77–100.

Halbritter, Bump. "Musical Rhetoric in the Integrated Media Composition." *Computers and Composition* 23.3 (2006): 317–34.

Haraway, Donna. *Simians, Cyborgs, and Women.* London: Routledge, 1991.

Harding, Sandra. *Whose Science? Whose Knowledge? Thinking from Women's Lives.* Ithaca, NY: Cornell UP, 1991.

Harris, Joseph. *A Teaching Subject: Composition since 1966.* Upper Saddle River, NJ: Prentice-Hall, 1997.

———. "Undisciplined Writing." *Delivering College Composition.* Ed. Kathleen Blake Yancey. Portsmouth, NH: Heinemann, 2006. 55–67.

———. "A Usable Past: *CCC* at 50." *College Composition and Communication* 50.4 (2009): 559–61.

Hawisher, Gail, Paul LeBlanc, Charles Moran, and Cynthia Selfe. *Computers and the Teaching of Writing in American Higher Education, 1979–1994: A History.* Norwood, NJ: Ablex, 1996.

Hawisher, Gail E., and Cynthia L. Selfe. "The Rhetoric of Technology and the Electronic Writing Class." *College Composition and Communication* 42.1 (1991): 55–65.

Hawk, Byron. *A Counter-History of Composition: Toward Methodologies of Complexity.* Pittsburgh: U of Pittsburgh P, 2007.

Henze, Brett, Jack Selzer, and Wendy Sharer. *1977: A Cultural Moment in Composition.* West Lafayette, IN: Parlor, 2008.

Hocks, Mary E. "Understanding Visual Rhetoric in Digital Writing Environments." *College Composition and Communication* 54.4 (2003): 629–56.

Hogan, Patrick Colm. *Cognitive Science, Literature, and the Arts: A Guide for Humanists.* London: Routledge, 2003.

Hull, Glynda A., and Mira-Lisa Katz. "Crafting an Agentive Self: Case Studies of Digital Storytelling." *Research in the Teaching of English* 41.1 (2006): 43–81.

Hutchinson, Helene D. *Mixed Bag: Artifacts from the Contemporary Culture.* Glenview, IL: Scott, Foresman, 1970.

"iBird Explorer" Aug. 29, 2011. <http://www.ibird.com>.

Inman, James A. *Computers and Writing: The Cyborg Era.* Mahwah, NJ: Earlbaum, 2004.

Janangelo, Joseph. "Joseph Cornell and the Artistry of Composing Persuasive Hypertexts." *College Composition and Communication* 49.1 (1998): 24–44.

Jenkins, Henry. *Convergence Culture: Where Old and New Media Collide.* New York: New York UP, 2009.

Johnson-Eilola, Johndan. *Datacloud: Toward a New Theory of Online Work.* Cresskill, NJ: Hampton , 2005.

Johnson-Eilola, Johndan, and Stuart Selber. "Plagiarism, Originality, Assemblage." *Computers and Composition* 24 (2007): 375–403.

Journet, Debra. "Inventing Myself in Multimodality: Encouraging Senior Faculty to Use Digital Media." *Computers and Composition* 24 (2007): 107–20.

Kalmbach, James. *The Computer and the Page: The Theory, History, and Pedagogy of Publishing, Technology, and the Classroom.* New York: Ablex, 1996.

Kent, Thomas, ed. *Post-Process Theory: Beyond the Writing Process Paradigm.* Carbondale: Southern Illinois UP, 1999.

King, Emily. "Thinking inside the Box: Aspen Revisited." *Looking Closer 5: Critical Writings on Graphic Design.* Ed. Michael Beirut, William Drenttel, and Steven Heller. 62–68.

Kinloch, Valerie Felita. "Revisiting the Promise of 'Students' Right to Their Own Language': Pedagogical Strategies." *College Composition and Communication* 57.1 (2005): 83–113.

Kirtley, Susan. "Students' Views on Technology and Writing: The Power of Personal History." *Computers and Composition* 22.2 (2005): 209–30.

Kitalong, Karla et al. "Variations on a Theme: The Technology Autobiography as a Versatile Writing Assignment." *Teaching Writing with Computers.* Ed. Pamela Takayoshi and Brian Huot. Boston: Houghton Mifflin, 2003. 219–33.

Kligerman, Jack. "Photography, Perception, and Composition." *College Composition and Communication* 28.2 (1977): 174–78.

Kosslyn, Stephen. *Image and Brain: The Resolution of the Imagery Debate.* Cambridge, MA: MIT P, 1996.

Kostyosj. "Katie Couric's Interview with Peter Griffin as Sarah Palin." *YouTube.* Mar. 1, 2010. Aug. 29, 2011. <http://www.youtube.com/user/kostyosj#p/u/2/VzPhhPDoD7w>.

Kress, Gunther. *Literacy in the New Media Age.* London: Routledge, 2003.

Kress, Gunther, and Theo Van Leeuwen. *Multimodal Discourse: The Modes and Media of Contemporary Communication.* London: Edward Arnold, 2001.

Kytle, Ray. *The Comp Box: A Writing Workshop Approach to College Composition.* New York: Aspen Communications, 1972.

Lambert, Joe. *Digital Storytelling: Capturing Lives: Creating Community.* Berkley, CA: Digital Diner, 2006.

Lee, Valerie, and Cynthia L. Selfe "Our Capacious Caper: Exposing Print-Culture Bias in Departmental Tenure Documents." *ADE Bulletin* 145 (2008): 51–58.

Lessig, Lawrence. "On Laws That Choke Creativity." *TED* Mar. 2007. Aug. 29, 2011. <http://www.ted.com/talks/larry_lessig_says_the_law_is_strangling_creativity.html>.

———. *Remix: Making Art and Commerce Thrive in the Hybrid Economy.* New York: Penguin, 2008.

Logie, John. *Peers, Pirates, and Persuasion: Rhetoric in the Peer-to-Peer Debates.* West Lafayette, IN: Parlor, 2006.

Lovett, Maria, et al. "Writing with Video: What Happens When Composition Comes off the Page?" *RAW (Reading and Writing) New Media.* Ed. Cheryl Ball and James Kalmbach. Creskill, NJ: Hampton, 2010. 287–304.

Lunsford, Andrea A. *Writing Matters: Rhetoric in Public and Private Lives.* Athens: U of Georgia P, 2007.

Lutz, William D. "Making Freshman English a Happening." *College Composition and Communication* 22 (1971): 35–38.

Mahoney, John, and John Schmittroth. *The Insistent Present.* Boston: Houghton Mifflin, 1970.

Mahony, Patrick. "McLuhan in Light of Classical Rhetoric." *College Composition and Communication* 20.1 (1969): 12–17.

Manovich, Lev. *The Language of New Media.* Cambridge, MA: MIT P, 2001.

Martindale, Colin. "Biological Bases of Creativity." *Handbook of Creativity.* Ed. Robert J. Steinberg. Cambridge: Cambridge UP, 1999.

McCorkle, Ben. "Harbingers of the Printed Page: Nineteenth-Century Theories of Delivery as Remediation." *Rhetoric Society Quarterly* 35.4 (2005): 25–49.

McKee, Heidi. "Sound Matters: Notes towards the Analysis and Design of Sound in Multimodal Web Texts." *Computers and Composition* 23.3 (2006): 335–54.

McLuhan, Marshall. *Understanding Media: The Extensions of Man.* Cambridge, MA: MIT P, 1994.

McLuhan, Marshall, and Quentin Fiore. *The Medium Is the Massage: An Inventory of Effects.* New York: Bantam, 1967.

Miller, Susan. *Textual Carnivals: The Politics of Composition.* Carbondale: Southern Illinois UP, 1991.

Moffett, James. *Teaching the Universe of Discourse.* Boston: Houghton, 1968.

Moran, Charles. "Access: The A-Word in Technology Studies." *Passions, Pedagogies, and Twenty-First-Century Technologies.* Ed. Gail E. Hawisher and Cynthia L. Selfe. Logan: Utah State UP, 1999. 205–20.

———. "Computers and Composition, 1983–2002: What We Have Hoped For." *Computers and Composition* 20.4 (2003): 343–58.

Moss, Beverly. *A Community Text Arises: A Literate Text and a Literacy Tradition in African-American Churches.* Creskill, NJ: Hampton, 2002.

Mountford, Roxanne. "A Century after the Divorce: Challenges to a Rapprochement between Speech Communication and English." *The Sage Handbook of Rhetorical Studies.* Ed. Andrea Lunsford. Los Angeles: Sage, 2009. 407–22.

Murphy, Sharon. "TV Footage in the Composition Classroom." *College Composition and Communication* 23.1 (1972): 51–53.

Murray, Donald M. *Write to Learn.* New York: Holt, Rinehart, and Winston, 1984.

Murray, Joddy. *Non-Discursive Rhetoric: Image and Affect in Multimodal Composition.* Albany: State U of New York P, 2009.

New London Group. "A Pedagogy of Multiliteracies: Designing Social Futures." *Multiliteracies: Designing Social Futures.* Ed. Bill Cope and Mary Kalantzis. London: Routledge, 1999.

Nichols, Bill. *Introduction to Documentary.* Bloomington: Indiana UP, 2001.

Paivio, Allan. *Mental Representations: A Dual Coding Approach.* Oxford: Oxford UP, 1986.

Palfrey, John, and Urs Gasser. *Born Digital: Understanding the First Generation of Digital Natives.* New York: Basic, 2008.

Parks, Stephen. *Class Politics: The Movement for Students' Right to Their Own Language.* Urbana, IL: NCTE, 1999.

Perl, Sondra. "Understanding Composing." *College Composition and Communication* 31.4 (1980): 363–69.

Prensky, Marc. "Digital Natives, Digital Immigrants." *On the Horizon* 9.5 (2001): 1–2.

Ratcliffe, Krista. *Rhetorical Listening: Identification, Gender, Whiteness.* Carbondale: Southern Illinois UP, 2005.

Reid, Alexander. "Tuning In: Infusing Media Networks into Professional Writing Curriculum." *Kairos: A Journal of Rhetoric, Technology, and Pedagogy* 12.2 (2008). Aug. 29, 2011. <http://kairos.technorhetoric.net/12.2/binder.html?praxis/reid/index.html>.

———. *The Two Virtuals: New Media and Composition.* West Lafayette, IN: Parlor, 2007.

Rice, Jeff. *The Rhetoric of Cool: Composition Studies and New Media.* Carbondale: Southern Illinois UP, 2007.

Richardson, Elaine. *African-American Literacies.* New York: Routledge, 2003.

Ridolfo, Jim, and Dànielle Nicole DeVoss. "Composing for Recomposition: Rhetorical Velocity and Delivery." *Kairos: A Journal of Rhetoric, Technology, and Pedagogy* 13.2 (2009). Aug. 29, 2011. <http://endora.wide.msu.edu/13.2/topoi/ridolfo_devoss/intro.html>.

Rife, Martine Courant. "The Fair Use Doctrine: History, Application, and Implications for (New Media) Writing Teachers." *Computers and Composition* 24.2 (2007): 154–78.

Roskelly, Hephzibah, and Kate Ronald. *Reason to Believe: Romanticism, Pragmatism, and the Teaching of Writing.* Albany: State U of New York P, 1998.

Ross, Heather. "Digital Video and Composition: Gauging the Promise of a Low-Maintenance, High-Reward Relationship." *Kairos: A Journal of Rhetoric, Technology, and Pedagogy* 8.1 (2003). Aug. 29, 2011. <http://kairos.technorhetoric.net/8.1/index.html>.

Sego, Lewis Paige. "Review: Multi-Media Textbooks." *College Composition and Communication* 22.1 (1971): 54–57.

Selber, Stuart. *Multiliteracies for a Digital Age.* Carbondale: Southern Illinois UP, 2004.

Selfe, Cynthia L. "The Movement of Air, the Breath of Meaning: Aurality and Multimodal Composing." *College Composition and Communication* 60.4 (2009): 616–63.

———, ed. *Multimodal Composition: Resources for Teachers.* Creskill, NJ: Hampton, 2007.

———. *Technology and Literacy in the Twenty-First Century: The Importance of Paying Attention.* Carbondale: Southern Illinois UP, 1999.

———. "Toward New Media Texts: Taking Up the Challenges of Visual Literacy." *Writing New Media: Theory and Applications for Expanding the Teaching of Composition.* Ed. Anne Frances Wysocki, et al. Logan: Utah State UP, 2004. 67–110.

Selfe, Cynthia L., and Gail E. Hawisher. *Literate Lives in the Information Age: Narratives of Literacy from the United States.* Mahwah, NJ: Earlbaum, 2004.

Selfe, Richard J., and Cynthia L. Selfe. "'Convince Me!' Valuing Multimodal Literacies and Composing Public Service Announcements." *Theory into Practice* 47 (2008): 83–92.

Shankar, Tara Rosenberger. "Speaking on the Record: A Theory of Composition." *Computers and Composition* 23.3 (2006): 374–93.

Shipka, Jody. "A Multimodal Task-Based Framework for Composing." *College Composition and Communication* 57.2 (2005): 277–306.

———. "Sound Engineering: Toward a Theory of Multimodal Soundedness." *Computers and Composition* 23.3 (2006): 355–73.

Shor, Ira. *Critical Teaching and Everyday Life.* Boston: South End, 1980.

Shor, Ira, and Paulo Freire. *A Pedagogy of Liberation: Dialogues on Transforming Education.* South Hadley, MA: Bergin and Garvey, 1987.

Sirc, Geoffrey. *English Composition as a Happening.* Logan: Utah State UP, 2002.

Skinner-Linnenberg, Virginia. *Dramatizing Writing: Re-Incorporating Delivery in the Classroom.* Mahwah, NJ: Earlbaum, 1997.

Slatin, John M. "The Art of ALT: Toward a More Accessible Web." *Computers and Composition* 18.1 (2001): 73–81.

Smagorinsky, Peter. *Expressions: Multiple Intelligences and the English Class.* Urbana, IL: NCTE, 1991.

Smit, David W. *The End of Composition Studies.* Carbondale: Southern Illinois UP, 2004.

Smitherman, Geneva. *Black Talk: Words and Phrases from the Hood to the Amen Corner.* New York: Houghton Mifflin, 2000.

———. "CCCC's Role in the Struggle for Language Rights." *College Composition and Communication* 50.3 (1999): 349–76.

———. "English Teacher, Why You Be Doing the Thangs You Don't Do?" *English Journal* 61.1 (1972): 59–65.

———. "Soul 'n Style." *English Journal* 63.2 (1974): 16–17.

———. "Soul 'n Style." *English Journal.* 63.5 (1974): 16–17.

———. *Talkin and Testifyin: The Language of Black America.* Boston: Houghton Mifflin, 1977.

———. *Word from the Mother: Language and African Americans.* New York: Routledge, 2006.

Smitherman, Geneva, and Victor Villanueva, eds. *Language Diversity in the Classroom: From Intention to Practice.* Carbondale: Southern Illinois UP, 2003.

Sommers, Nancy. "Revision Strategies of Student Writers and Experienced Adult Writers." *College Composition and Communication* 31.4 (1980): 378–88.

Sorapure, Madeleine. "Five Principles of New Media: Or, Playing Lev Manovich." *Kairos: A Journal of Rhetoric, Technology, and Pedagogy* 8.2. (2003). Aug. 29, 2011. <http://english.ttu.edu/kairos/8.2/binder2.html?coverweb/sorapure/index.htm>.

Sparke, William, and Clark McKowen. *Montage: Investigations in Language.* New York: Macmillan, 1970.

———. *Teacher's Manual to Accompany Montage: Investigations in Language.* New York: Macmillan, 1970.

Stafford, Andrew, ed. "Aspen: The Multimedia Magazine in a Box." *UbuWeb* May 1, 2010. Aug. 29, 2011. <http://www.ubu.com/aspen/>.

Sullivan, Patricia, and James E. Porter. *Opening Spaces: Writing Technologies and Critical Research Practices.* Westport, CT: Ablex, 1997.

Takayoshi, Pamela, and Cynthia L. Selfe. "Thinking about Multimodality." *Multimodal Composition: Resources for Teachers.* Ed. Cynthia L. Selfe. Creskill, NJ: Hampton, 2008. 1–12.

Turner, Mark, ed. *The Artful Mind: Cognitive Science and the Riddle of Human Creativity.* Oxford: Oxford UP, 2006.

Ulmer, Gregory L. *Heuretics: The Logic of Invention.* Baltimore: Johns Hopkins UP, 1994.

Vertov, Dziga. *Kino-Eye: The Writings of Dziga Vertov.* Berkeley: U of California P, 1984.

Vie, Stephanie. "Digital Divide 2.0: 'Generation M' and Online Social Network Sites in the Composition Classroom." *Computers and Composition* 25.1 (2008). 9–23.

Wallas, Graham. *The Art of Thought.* New York: Harcourt Brace Jovanovich, 1926.

Wible, Scott. "Pedagogies of the 'Students' Rights' Era: The Language Curriculum Research Group's Project for Linguistic Diversity." *College Composition and Communication* 57.3 (2006): 442–78.

WIDE Research Center Collective. "Why Teach Digital Writing?" *Kairos* 10.1 (2005). Aug. 29, 2011. <http://english.ttu.edu/KAIROS/10.1/binder2.html?coverweb/wide/index.html>.

Wiener, Harvey S. "Media Compositions: Preludes to Writing." *College English* 35.5 (1974): 566–74.

Williamson, Richard. "The Case for Filmmaking as English Composition." *College Composition and Communication* 22.2 (1971): 131–36.

Wilson, R. N. "Poetic Creativity, Process, and Personality." *Psychiatry* 17.2 (1954): 163–76.

Winchester, Otis. *The Sound of Your Voice.* Boston: Allyn and Bacon, 1972.

Wysocki, Anne Frances. "With Eyes That Think, and Compose, and Think: On Visual Rhetoric." *Teaching Writing with Computers: An Introduction.* Ed. Pamela Takayoshi and Brian Huot. Boston: Houghton Mifflin, 2003. 182–201.

Wysocki, Anne Frances, et al. *Writing New Media: Theory and Applications for Expanding the Teaching of Composition.* Logan: Utah State UP, 2004.

Xerox. Advertisement. College Composition and Communication 24.1 (1973): 11.

Yancey, Kathleen Blake. "Made Not Only in Words: Composition in a New Key." *College Composition and Communication* 56.2 (2004): 297–328.

Zdenek, Sean. "Accessible Podcasting: College Students on the Margins in the New Media Classroom." *Computers and Composition Online* Fall 2009. Aug. 29, 2011. <http://seanzdenek.com/?page_id=22>.

INDEX

access, 11, 170n7
acting, 53, 63–65
administration, 152–53
African American language practices, 54; oral storytelling, 75–76
African Americans, 11, 54
African American Vernacular English, 72–74, 167–68n3
age, assumptions about, 113–14
allied arts, 27–28, 39–40, 151; student exercises, 48–50
alphabetic writing: as auditory technology, 55; as collaborative auditory process, 68; as creative problem-solving process, 29–30; filmmaking and, 130–37, 143–45; as heritage, 4–6; imagery, role of, 8–9; limitations of, 34, 36, 46–48, 143, 145, 158–59; as multimodal process, 5–6, 9, 16–17, 25, 32, 44–46; as nonlinear process, 17, 27, 40; oral traditions and, 74; performing out loud, 64–65; photography and reinvention of, 141–43; as recursive process, 27–30; as shape/structure, 35; speech deeply interconnected with, 79–81; strategies for inventing and revising, 149–52; as translation, 26; as visual-kinesthetic art, 123; visual thinking as analogous to, 39
analog technologies, 6, 17–18, 87–89, 126–27; cassette slideshow project, 97–99; media collages, 105, 108; super 8 camera, 140–41; talking books,

54, 69–70; tape recorders, 57–58. *See also* photography
Angell, C. F., 128–29
Aristotle, 1, 92–93
Arnheim, Rudolph, 38
arrangement, 133–36
Ashton-Warner, Sylvia, 43
Aspen Communications, 106, 169n4
assemblage, 90, 103–8, 111–12
associative linking, 11–12, 31
associative practices, 87, 89, 100–108, 111–12
associative remix, 13, 16. *See also* remix
Audacity (software), 56, 58, 70
audience, 49; adapting discourses to, 61, 62; communicative competence and, 77; dialogue and, 69; ethos, construction of, 62, 81; remix of compositions, 70
audience analysis: classical rhetorical theories, 92–93; spoken performance and, 53, 64
auditory composition, 10, 17, 53, 82
auditory forms of communication: dialect, 17, 54, 72–79, 167–68n3; dialogue, 17, 54, 65–72, 81; scholarship on, 52–53. *See also* speech; voice
auditory thinking, 51–52
aurality, 7
authorship, concepts of, 106, 107

banking model of education, 66, 80, 127

187

Jason Palmeri is an assistant professor of English and affiliate faculty in interactive media studies at Miami University in Oxford, Ohio, where he also serves as coordinator of the Digital Writing Collaborative. He has published numerous articles in journals such as *Computers and Composition* and *Technical Communication Quarterly*.

CCCC STUDIES IN WRITING & RHETORIC

Edited by Joseph Harris, Duke University

The aim of the CCCC Studies in Writing & Rhetoric (SWR) series is to influence how writing gets taught at the college level. The methods of studies vary from the critical to historical to linguistic to ethnographic, and their authors draw on work in various fields that inform composition—including rhetoric, communication, education, discourse analysis, psychology, cultural studies, and literature. Their focuses are similarly diverse—ranging from individual writers and teachers to classrooms and communities and curricula, to analyses of the social, political, and material contexts of writing and its teaching. Still, all SWR volumes try in some way to inform the practice of writing students, teachers, or administrators. Their approach is synthetic, their style concise and pointed. Complete manuscripts run from 40,000 to 50,000 words, or about 150–200 pages. Authors should imagine their work in the hands of writing teachers, as well as on library shelves.

SWR was one of the first scholarly book series to focus on the teaching of writing. It was established in 1980 by the Conference on College Composition and Communication (CCCC) to promote research in the emerging field of writing studies. Since its inception, the series has been copublished by Southern Illinois University Press. As the field has grown, the research sponsored by SWR has continued to articulate the commitment of CCCC to supporting the work of writing teachers as reflective practitioners and intellectuals. For a list of previous SWR books, see the SWR link on the SIU Press website at www.siupress.com.

We are eager to identify influential work in writing and rhetoric as it emerges. We thus ask authors to send us project proposals that clearly situate their work in the field and show how they aim to redirect our ongoing conversations about writing and its teaching. Proposals should include an overview of the project, a brief annotated table of contents, and a sample chapter. They should not exceed 10,000 words.

To submit a proposal or to contact the series editor, please go to http://uwp.aas.duke.edu/cccc/swr/.

OTHER BOOKS IN THE CCCC STUDIES IN WRITING & RHETORIC SERIES